Turbo Database Toolbox

Owner's Handbook

Copyright

BORLAND INTERNA
4585 Scotts
Scotts Valle

TABLE OF CONTENTS

Appendices

LIST OF FIGURES

INTRODUCTION

This book is a reference manual for the Turbo Database Toolbox (formerly called the Turbo Toolbox), implemented for the CP/M-80, CP/M-86 and MS-DOS operating systems. The Turbo Database Toolbox consists of a set of three programs (tools) that can help you develop and streamline your Turbo Pascal programs.

This manual makes extensive use of Turbo Pascal programming examples; a good working knowledge of Turbo Pascal is assumed. If you need to brush up on your Pascal knowledge, refer to the *Turbo Pascal Reference Manual* and/or the *Turbo Tutor*.

What Can You Do With the Database Toolbox?

The Turbo Database Toolbox gives you three tools that make for fast and easy development of Turbo Pascal programs:

- The Turbo Access system
- The Turbo Sort system
- The GINST general installation system

These tools are provided in modular form, so they can be included as needed in your Pascal programs for the benefit of your end users.

The Turbo Access System

The Turbo Access system is a way to efficiently store and retrieve information contained in large data files. Turbo Access retrieves information either randomly by key (instead of just a number), or in sorted sequence.

Turbo Access speeds up the typically slow, laborious record searching process by using key strings to form relationships between data files and index files. The key strings are stored independently of the data, and usually represent some important aspect of the information being stored or sought—for instance, a customer's name, or a product's stock number. Since your computer needn't search through the whole database in sequential order, it's easy to quickly locate, insert, or delete a data record when you need to.

The method of indexing used by the Turbo Access system is the *B + tree*. More detailed information on *B + trees* can be found in Appendix B. However, you don't need to understand B + trees to use the Database Toolbox, and if you'd like to get right down to the nitty gritty of searching and sorting, you can turn directly to Chapter 2 and get started right away.

The Turbo Sort System

The Turbo Sort system uses the popular *Quicksort* algorithm to ensure fast and efficient sorting of your data files. With this tool, you can sort any type of data either on a single item or on multiple keys. You can also sort different data items in the same program. Turbo Sort's virtual memory management automatically uses the disk to expand sorting space if the file to be sorted is too big for your computer's RAM memory.

GINST—General Installation System

GINST solves one of the biggest problems facing programmers: how to get programs up and running on different terminals. GINST lets you develop an installation module identical to Turbo Pascal's, without having to worry about writing terminal-specific installation programs yourself. By simply answering a few questions asked by the GINST program, end users can easily install your programs for their particular terminals.

Structure of This Manual

This manual is divided into six parts:

- Chapter 1 introduces you to the Database Toolbox. We'll define the basic terms you need to know to understand this manual, and give you a concrete example of how you might use the Database Toolbox.

- Chapter 2 gets you started right away on using the Turbo Database Toolbox. This chapter includes Turbo Pascal program examples for both basic and advanced applications. All the examples in this chapter are included on your distribution diskette.

- Chapter 3 is the technical reference part of the manual. All the constants, procedures and functions contained in the Turbo Access system are described in alphabetical order, with parameters, function, restrictions and examples.

- Chapter 4 tells you how to use GINST—the General Installation system—to develop installation modules for your programs.

- Appendix A, Tips for Toolbox Programmers, contains some handy suggestions for writing good Turbo Access programs.

- Appendix B describes the B+tree structure used by the Turbo Access system. Although you don't need to understand B+trees to use the Database Toolbox, if you are an experienced programmer you may be interested in knowing more about how Turbo Access works.

- Appendix C provides an ASCII conversion table for quick reference.

If you want to get your application program up and running as quickly as possible, read the tutorial and examples in Chapter 2, and ignore the subtleties of B+trees. If you are an expert programmer and want to know exactly how Turbo Access works so you can "tune" it for maximum efficiency for your application, read Appendix B.

Typography

The body of this manual is printed in normal typeface. Special characters are used for the following special purposes:

Alternate   Alternate characters are used in program examples and procedure and function declarations.

Italics   *Italics are used to emphasize certain concepts and terminology, such as predefined standard identifiers, parameters, and other syntax elements.*

Boldface   **Boldface type is used to mark reserved words, in the text as well as in program examples.**

Refer to the *Turbo Pascal Reference Manual* for a complete description of the syntax, special characters and overall appearance of the Pascal language.

The Distribution Diskette

The Turbo Database Toolbox distribution diskette contains several files related to each tool. The file names belonging to each tool are provided in Chapter 3. Your diskette contains:

- A sample database, BTREE.PAS, that utilizes the Turbo Access system
- Source code for Turbo Access and Turbo Sort
- The SETCONST.PAS program for helping you set Turbo Access constants
- The TBDEMO.PAS Toolbox demonstration program
- The GINST (General Installation) program
- Files containing all procedures and functions
- All the commented program examples in the manual

See the READ.ME file on your distribution diskette for a complete listing of the files in the Turbo Database Toolbox package.

The distribution diskette is your only source for the Turbo Database Toolbox files. The first thing you should do upon receiving the diskette is to complete and mail the License Agreement at the front of this manual. You should then make a copy of the distribution diskette. Put the original diskette in a safe place, and use only the copy for doing your work. You should never use the distribution diskette, since there is a charge for a replacement copy.

Acknowledgments

In this manual, references are made to several products:

- SideKick is a registered trademark of Borland International
- Turbo Pascal is a registered trademark of Borland International
- WordStar is a registered trademark of MicroPro International
- CP/M is a registered trademark of Digital Research
- MS-DOS is a trademark of Microsoft

Chapter 1
A TOOLBOX PRIMER

The Turbo Database Toolbox is extremely easy to use. As long as you know something about writing Turbo Pascal programs, you can pop the Database Toolbox diskette into your computer and start streamlining your application programs immediately, without having to know anything about the inner workings of the program.

There are, however, a few terms and concepts used throughout this manual that you need to know to understand the Turbo Access part of the Toolbox. This chapter defines those terms and concepts. And in case you're a little fuzzy about just how the Toolbox can help you with the programming and database management tasks you're up against, we open this chapter with a real-life example of how you might put the Toolbox to work for you.

What's Turbo Access Good For? The Saga of Dr. Flossmore

A dentist, Dr. U. Flossmore, has a small dental practice. He has an IBM PC with 128K, two 360K disk drives and a copy of Turbo Pascal. He would like to use his computer to help keep track of his patients.

He had spent $695 on a well-known database program for this purpose, but since it turned out to be so much work to customize the program to his particular needs, he decided it would be easier to write a Turbo Pascal program from scratch.

Dr. Flossmore looked at the factors involved in writing his own programs to keep track of his patients. For every patient, he needed to keep track of name, address, telephone number, how much owed on account, state of dental health, and a few other odds and ends. A typical patient record might be:

John Smith
123 Plum Alley
Boston, Mass.
unlisted
root canal, tooth #19
check gums on tooth #2 next time

likes nitrous oxide
check on flossing next time
account paid up

In Dr. Flossmore's case, the total amount of information required for each patient would never exceed 300 characters, so it could be put into a record consisting of 300 bytes. The entire database for 1000 patients would thus require 300 x 1000 bytes, or 300K, neatly fitting on one diskette.

How should all this data be organized on the disk? The simplest way would be to store it sequentially, all in one big file. The first patient typed in would occupy the first 300 bytes, the next patient the next 300 bytes, and so on. New patients would just be added to the end of the file. This is very simple and easy to program in Turbo Pascal, but it also makes accessing patient records very inefficient. Suppose, for example, Mr. Smith calls to make an appointment. It is no big deal to search through 300K of internal RAM memory for a given name, but it will take about a minute for an IBM PC to search through a diskette for a name. Knowing that Mr. Smith doesn't like to be kept waiting, Dr. Flossmore needs a faster solution.

Another approach might be to write all the records out on index cards, sort them in alphabetical order, and then enter them on the disk in alphabetical order. A clever program could then be much more efficient about finding a given name on the disk, and could do it in about five seconds. Besides the obvious nuisances of sorting the index cards and writing the clever disk access program, this approach provides no good way to handle new patients. If Dr. Flossmore has patients named Smith and Smithy, they would be stored next to each other on the disk and there would be no room in the alphabetical sequence for a new patient named Smithson.

A more sophisticated approach would be to partition the disk in portions reserved for different alphabetical groups. For example, a big block of disk space could be reserved for patients whose names begin with the letter A, another block for the letter B, and so on. A strategy like this would work for a while, but after a few months, it is likely that the addition of new patients would cause certain letters like "S" to "fill up"; the result would be no more room in the "S" block for patients' names beginning with the letter "S."

The problem of organizing the patients' records on the disk is much more complicated than it appears at first glance. Fortunately, however, there is a nice solution to the problem: Turbo Access.

Here's how Dr. Flossmore can use Turbo Access to solve the problem of cataloguing his patient records on his PC. All he has to do is define a Turbo Pascal record that will be the structure for his 300-byte patient records, and get his data into that format. Turbo Access does the rest.

Turbo Access stores records on disk in a very clever format using *B + trees*. It then provides the three functions that Dr. Flossmore really needs:

- Retrieves a patient record from the disk
- Adds a patient record to the disk
- Deletes a patient record from the disk

Turbo Access maintains a complicated set of tables on the disk that allow for the efficient access of records. Each time a patient record is added or deleted from the disk, these tables are automatically updated so that the program continues to be efficient, both in terms of memory usage and record access times. The result is that Dr. Flossmore can easily maintain his patient database of 1000 patients on his diskette, and access a given patient's record in about two seconds. Furthermore, he can add and delete thousands of patients, with no significant change in performance.

Some Words You'll Want to Know

The following sections define the fundamental concepts you need to know to read this manual and use Turbo Access. We're only giving you the bare bones in this chapter; if you run across other terms you don't understand as you read this manual, check Appendix B, "B + tree Structure."

Data Files

Data files are simply that—files that contain data. As a Turbo Database Toolbox user, the kinds of data files you are probably most interested in are files that contain some kind of database—a set of interrelated data, such as names and addresses of all the employees in a company—that you want to access or sort alphabetically. In the Turbo Database Toolbox, a data file is made up of up to 65,535 *records*.

Records

The separate, yet interrelated pieces of information that make up a data file are *records.* For instance, in a database made up of customers who have an account in a department store, one customer's name, address, phone number, and account status would constitute one record in the data file. Organizing a data file into separate units—records—makes it possible to perform the tasks that are routine to managing a database: adding and deleting names from that database, finding a given customer's name to update his or her account status, or keeping all the names in alphabetical order. The Turbo Database Toolbox lets you perform these tasks by way of *keys* contained in *index files.*

Index Files

Index files are analogous to data files; they also are made up of separate pieces of information. However, index files are not made up of the data in your database; instead, they consist of up to 65,535 *keys.* Turbo Access uses the keys, stored in index files, to manage the records contained in your data files.

Keys

Keys are what Turbo Access uses to unlock (access and operate on) your database. A key is a string of characters that is related to one record in the database. For easy reference, a key is usually based on some important element (a *field*) in the record. For instance, a key for a customer record in the department store database mentioned above might be the customer's last name or account number.

How Index Files and Data Files Relate

Index files and data files are usually stored together on some storage device—a hard or floppy disk—but they are entirely distinct from each other. Turbo Access—via its B+tree structure—goes back and forth between the two types of files, using a key string associated with a data record. In addition, every data record is assigned a unique number (the *data reference*) by Turbo Access, so that even if there are duplicate keys (which is a common occurrence in a large database that contains several people with identical last names), the correct data record can still be located by Turbo Access.

It is possible for one record to be accessed by several keys. For instance, one index file might be made up of keys relating to those customers who spend more than $500 per month in the department store; the keys would be based on numbers of 500 and greater (See Chapter 2, page 21 for how to convert numeric keys to alphabetic keys). These keys could be used to locate customers who the department store manager wants to target for a special "preferred customer" mailing. Another index file might consist of keys relating to those customers who are behind on paying their accounts, to be targeted for another, persuasive type of mailing. Another index file could consist of keys based simply on the customers' last names. In short, the exact relationship between a data file and its related index file(s) is up to you; Turbo Access is designed so that you can work flexibly with the information contained in your database.

You can see that Turbo Access is very much like a reference librarian: when adding a new book to the library, the librarian must also add a card in the catalogue. To find a book (record) that interests you, you simply ask the librarian—Turbo Access—to look up the book (record) in the card catalogue (index file), get the book's number (data reference) and retrieve the book (record) for you.

As you can see, the concepts are simple. Now you're ready to move on to doing some work with the Database Toolbox.

Notes:

Chapter 2
GETTING STARTED

This chapter gets you off to a quick start with the Turbo Database Toolbox. Using commented program examples, we'll show you how to wield each tool with ease and finesse, beginning with Turbo Access, followed by Turbo Sort. GINST, the general installation system, is covered in Chapter 4.

This chapter begins with an overview of Turbo Access. Next, we present an example of how to use Turbo Access in a common programming situation—how to use it to add and delete data records and keys. The example is based on the BTREE.PAS customer database included on your distribution diskette. Finally, you'll learn how to use Turbo Sort to sort your data on both single items and multiple keys.

All of the sample programs in this chapter are included on your distribution diskette, so you can try them out and experiment with the calling parameters in the various procedures. Each sample program is listed under a file name of the form FILENAME.PAS.

This chapter is designed as a basic tutorial. Technical details about the Turbo Database Toolbox procedures and functions used in this chapter can be found in Chapter 3. Appendix B contains information about the B+tree structure used by Turbo Access.

Including Turbo Database Routines in Your Programs

Both Turbo Access and Turbo Sort are supplied on the disk in readable source code that you are free to use any way you like. You can include the modules in your own Turbo Pascal programs, without ever taking a look at the source code, and without worrying about how it works. You can study the source code to learn from it, or you can even make your own changes to it. But remember, if you alter the source code, you are as much on your own as if you had written the entire program yourself; our technical support staff will be unable to help you should problems arise. Also, while you may distribute a program that *includes* Turbo Access or Turbo Sort, you may not distribute the modules themselves as standalone products.

To use the Turbo Database Toolbox, you must first incorporate the source file modules you need for your application program with the Turbo Pascal *include directive*. The include directive is a comment that tells the compiler to read the program contained in the specified file. This directive starts with *$I*, followed by the file name and optional three-letter extension of the file to be included. To be understood by the Turbo Database compiler, the entire include directive must be enclosed within braces, i.e., { *$I filename.EXT*}. For more information about the include directive, see Chapter 1 in the *Turbo Pascal Reference Manual*.

Using Turbo Access

Turbo Access is a tool that allows you to quickly access, search, and administer large data files used by Turbo Pascal programs. Turbo Access uses *keys*—code words based on some important aspect of your data—to quickly locate, add or delete data records, without requiring a sequential search through the entire data file.

Every Turbo Database Toolbox program that uses Turbo Access must include either the ACCESS2.BOX module (for Turbo Pascal 2.0) or ACCESS3.BOX module (for Turbo Pascal 3.0), and it must be included first. These files contain the basic data and index file setup and maintenance routines; Turbo Pascal 3.0 handles file I/O somewhat differently than Turbo Pascal 2.0. You should rename the module you are using to ACCESS.BOX.

As explained, the ACCESS routines are different for Turbo Pascal versions 2.0 and 3.0:

- Turbo Pascal 2.0: Run TURBO2.BAT to install Turbo Database Toolbox.

- Turbo Pascal 3.0: Use ACCESS.BOX on this version—no installation is required.

Note: This information applies to 16-bit systems only. No special installation is required for CP/M-80 Toolbox users and only one ACCESS.BOX file is included on the distribution disk. CP/M-86 users should rename ACCESS.BOX to ACCESS3.BOX and rename ACCESS2.BOX to ACCESS.BOX.

Next, you must include the module(s) needed for your particular application. These modules can be included in any order, and you need only include the modules you require. The modules can also be used in program overlays. The modules are as follows:

- ACCESS.BOX contains the basic data and index file setup and maintenance routines.
- GETKEY.BOX contains the Turbo Access search routines *NextKey*, *PrevKey*, *FindKey*, and *SearchKey*.
- ADDKEY.BOX contains the *AddKey* procedure used for inserting keys into index files.
- DELKEY.BOX contains the *DeleteKey* procedure used for deleting keys from index files.

Before including the ACCESS.BOX module, you must declare some integer constants to determine the configuration of the B+tree structure. The values of the constants affect search speed and the amount of memory (RAM and index file) used by the Turbo Access system.

A program, SETCONST.PAS, is provided on your distribution diskette to help you set the values of these constants. To use it, load and compile the program; then run the program and answer the questions it asks you. You will be asked for the maximum size of your data records, the maximum key length, and the maximum number of keys you will be using. You can experiment with the values, and SET-CONST.PAS will show you how the values you specify affect other values. When you have determined the values you want for the constants, you can output the result of your interaction with SET-CONST.PAS as a text file that will contain all your constant declarations.

The SETCONST.PAS program is included in this Turbo Database Toolbox package to make it easy for you to set constant values without having to know the nitty gritty details about B+trees. For those of you who are interested in the technicalities of Toolbox constants, see Chapter 3.

SETCONST requires you to enter five inputs:

- Data record size (*MaxDataRecSize*)
- Key length (*MaxKeyLen*)
- An estimate of the number of records that will be in the file

- The page size in keys (*PageSize*)
- Page stack size in pages (*PageStackSize*)

Once given these values, SETCONST calculates several outputs; each output is given three times, once each for a database that is 50%, 75% and 100% full. The density of the database depends on how it's created (the order of insertion of new items), and tends to be about 75%. The outputs are:

- Total index file pages—the number of index file pages necessary to hold the index at the given density.
- *Order*—constant required by Turbo Access.
- *MaxHeight*—constant required by Turbo Access. This value depends partly on density of the database. For safety, the highest value listed for *MaxHeight* (automatically displayed by SET-CONST) should be used.
- Memory used for page stack—amount of RAM memory used by the page stack.
- Index file page size—size, in bytes, of a single page in the index file (how large individual reads and writes of the index will be).
- Index file size—approximate size of the entire index file.
- Data file size—approximate size of the entire data file.
- Average searches needed to find a key—average number of times that the index file must be searched to locate a particular key.
- Average searches satisfied by page stack—when searching for a key, some of the index pages needed for the search will be in the page stack.
- Average disk searches needed to find a key—number of searches that will remain after the page stack has been exhausted.

The first three inputs (data record size, key length, size of the database) should be known beforehand; the corresponding default values for *PageSize* and *PageStackSize* are acceptable for most applications. *PageSize* and *PageStackSize* should be varied to minimize the number of (slow) disk searches needed to find a key, while not wasting too much memory for the page stack. The significance of the four most important outputs is as follows:

1) Memory used for page stack—as value increases, more memory is used
2) Index file size—as value increases, more disk space is used

3) Data file size—as value increases, more disk space is used
4) Average disk searches needed to find a key—as value increases, more time is used

Other constants are not important or are incorporated into these.

Increasing *PageSize* or *PageStackSize* will always increase #1 and #2 while decreasing #4. A balance must be found where the number of disk searches needed is low, while the amount of memory used is also low; the importance of memory and disk space depends on the application. #3 is affected only by the data record size and the size of the database, so there is little that can be done to minimize it.

When you have decided on all the values, press Escape to end the program. It will ask you whether to write the constants out to a file; if you say yes, it will ask you for the file name, then write out the constants in this form:

```
const
  MaxDataRecSize = 200;
  MaxKeyLen = 10;
  PageSize = 24;
  Order = 12;
  PageStackSize = 10;
  MaxHeight = 4;
```

Warning: Care must be taken when specifying the size of your keys, records, and constants. You should never count the bytes manually. Instead, use the *SizeOf* function to determine the actual size of your data structure and then type this value into your Toolbox program. (See page 20 of the Owner's Handbook for more discussion.)

For example:

```
program ShowSize;

type
  KeyString = string[25];
  CustRec = record
    Name : KeyString;
    Balance : real;
  end;                                          { CustRec }

begin
  Writeln(SizeOf('MaxKeyLen=',SizeOf(KeyString)-1);
  Writeln('MaxDataRecSize=',SizeOf(CustRec));
end.
```

If you were to count the bytes manually in this example, you would incorrectly add 25 (your string length) to your 6-byte real number and declare:

```
const
  MaxDataRecSize = 31;
  MaxKeyLen      = 25;
    .
    .
    .
```

These sizes are incorrect! Turbo Pascal strings range from 0 to their defined length. In the example above, *Name* is actually 26 bytes long. Perhaps you are using the Turbo Pascal BCD or 8087 compiler—both of which feature longer real numbers (10 and 8 bytes respectively).

To further avoid errors, your program should also pass *SizeOf* (CustRec) to the *MakeFile* and *OpenFile* procedures instead of an integer constant:

```
MakeFile(DataF, 'CUST.DTA', SizeOf(CustRec));
OpenFile(DataF, 'CUST.DTA', SizeOf(CustRec));
```

Data Files

A Turbo Access data file can contain up to 65,536 records. This includes a reserved record and all deleted records. However, only one system record (record 0) is reserved, and deleted records are reused before the file is expanded. This effectively allows for 65,535 user records.

The size of a data record, in theory, can be up to 64K bytes. However, a record that large would allow only about 160 records to be stored on a 10 megabyte hard disk (with no index files). It is good practice to try to minimize the size of the data record by using codes and abbreviations. Though large records will not affect search times, they do tend to fill up disks. The smallest data record allowed is 8 bytes, and the data record size is fixed for any given data file.

In contrast to ordinary Turbo Pascal data files, the Turbo Access data file variables are always declared using the *DataFile* type (in the ACCESS.BOX module). The file record size is determined at run time by parameters passed to the *MakeFile* or *OpenFile* procedure.

Index Files

The maximum number of entries in an index file is the same as the number of records in a data file, 65,535. It is the user program's responsibility to designate key information and to provide it and the data record number to the index update routine *AddKey.*

One data file can be referenced by several index files. This allows one set of data to be keyed using different aspects of the data record. In addition, keys may or may not be part of the actual data record. However, we recommend that a key be a field in the actual data record, or be computed from one or more fields in the record. If you include the key elements in the data record, you can rebuild an index that has been lost or corrupted.

For example, suppose your application program is designed to maintain a mailing list. The keys stored in the index could be the last name of each entry in the data file, converted to uppercase. If a search string is also converted to uppercase, Turbo Access will find the appropriate entry—regardless of whether it was entered using uppercase and lowercase letters—but the data record will still retain the data exactly as entered. In general, key values should always be duplicated in the data file records unless you have a very limited amount of disk storage.

The disk space used by an index file is determined by the key length and the number of records that are indexed and the order of insertion. Experiment with the SETCONST.PAS program (page setconst) to obtain the appropriate values for your application. If you want to minimize the size of index files, the best place to start is with the key length.

Program Structure with Turbo Access

In most cases, your application program will use Turbo Access to perform one or more of the following functions:

- Add data records

- Retrieve data records

- Update data records

- Delete data records

In addition, prior to processing any data, an application program must prepare (open) the necessary index and data files, and at termination, close these files.

Initializing the User Program

The initialization phase consists of calling either *MakeFile* (for a new file) or *OpenFile* (for an existing file) for each data file to be used, and *MakeIndex* (new) or *OpenIndex* (existing) for each index file. In addition, *InitIndex* must be called to initialize the index file manager routines. *InitIndex* tells Turbo Access that there are no open index files, and clears the page stack buffer so that none of the information it contains is written to the index files. *InitIndex* must only be called once at the beginning of a program that uses index files; it must never be called twice in the same program, since any currently open index files would be corrupted.

User Program Variables

The Turbo Access modules contain a number of internal variables. To avoid duplication of their names in your user programs, they all begin with the characters "TA". This does not *prevent* you from using variables that start with "TA", but can result in compiler error number 43: "Duplicate identifier or label" if you do use these variable names.

Error Handling

Turbo Access routines generate two types of errors: non-fatal errors and fatal errors. Fatal errors cause the program to terminate, while non-fatal errors are simply reported to the program through the Boolean variable *OK*, which is automatically declared by the ACCESS.BOX module. For instance, *OpenFile* returns FALSE in *OK* if the specified file was not found and *FindKey* returns FALSE if the key string was not found.

If a fatal error occurs, a routine called *TalOcheck* (in the ACCESS.BOX module) is invoked. It displays an error code, a file name, and a record number, and then terminates the program. The following is an example of an error display:

```
Turbo-file I.O error 10
File A:CUST.DAT Record 103
Program terminated
```

A Turbo Access fatal error is equivalent to a Turbo Pascal I/O error. Possible error codes are therefore the same as those listed in the *Turbo Pascal Reference Manual*. However, Turbo Access outputs the error code in decimal, while Turbo Pascal outputs it in hexadecimal.

The following table converts the error numbers to the I/O listed in the manual. (The last error described by this table actually applies to Turbo Pascal 3.0 users only.)

IOresult#		Error message from Turbo Pascal manual
1	90	Record length mismatch
2	01	File does not exist
3	F1	Directory is full
4	04	File not open
5	02	File not open for input
6	03	File not open for output
7	99	Unexpected end-of-file
8	F0	Disk write error
9	10	Error in numeric format
10	99	Unexpected end-of-file
14	F2	File size overflow
12	99	Unexpected end-of-file
13	F0	Disk write error
14	91	Seek beyond end-of-file
15	04	File not open
16	20	Operation not allowed on a logical device
17	21	Not allowed in direct mode
18	22	Assign to std files not allowed
144	90	Record length mismatch
145	91	Seek beyond end-of-file
153	99	Unexpected end-of-file
240	F0	Disk write error
243	F3	Too many files open (Turbo Pascal 3.0 only)

In general, fatal errors occur only when a data and/or index file is corrupted. A fatal error also occurs if you try to expand a data file or an index file when there is insufficient disk space.

User Program Termination

At termination, your program must call *CloseFile* for each data file in use, and *CloseIndex* for each index file. If a file is created but not closed, or closed but has zero records, the file cannot be used until it is deleted or rewritten.

Some Database Tasks: Quick Summary

The following sections give you a quick rundown on how to handle some basic database tasks: adding and deleting records and keys, locating key values, and handling numeric and duplicate keys. Complete program examples can be found later in this chapter.

Adding Data Records

To add a data record, first input the record, and then add it to the data file with the *AddRec* procedure. *AddRec* returns a record number that should be stored in a temporary variable. Then choose a key value from one or more fields of the data record. Now pass the key and the record number to the *AddKey* routine. If your program maintains more than one index, call *AddKey* for each index file, passing the same record number each time. If your index file does not allow duplicates, you should always check the status variable *OK* after each call to *AddKey* (see page 21 for how Turbo Access handles duplicate keys).

Key Location

To locate a key value, use the *FindKey, SearchKey, NextKey* and *Prev-Key* routines to search the index (or indexes). Once the key has been found, use *GetRec* to obtain the associated data record from the data file. Note that the key field in the *FindKey* and *SearchKey* procedures is a variable parameter. If you search for a customer named *Smith* and the key is not found, for example:

```
FindKey(IndexF, DataRef, Name);
```

the global variable *OK* will be set to FALSE and the value of *Name* will have been destroyed (it is actually set to the value of the last key read from the index file). Always use a scratch variable (or parameter) in your search routine, as shown in the following example.

```
Write('Enter name to find: ');
Read(Name);
Scratch := Name;  { Scratch is same type as Name }
FindKey(IndexF, DataRef, Scratch);
if not OK then
  Writeln(' - Sorry:  I cannot find ', Name);
```

Deleting Data Records

To delete a data record, first find its key with *FindKey, SearchKey, NextKey* or *PrevKey,* as just described. Then call *DeleteKey* to delete the record from the index file. If there is more than one index, read the data record (*GetRec*), and derive from it the keys to be deleted from the other index files. Finally, call *DeleteRec* to remove the data record from the data file.

If your index file allows duplicates, you must also pass the data record number of the key you want to delete by saving the record number that is returned by *FindKey, SearchKey, NextKey* or *PrevKey.* Then, when you call *DeleteKey,* pass it the key and the record number.

Key Change

Changes made to a data record may affect the key value(s). For example, a person might change his name from "Carroll" to "James." If so, you must call *DeleteKey* to delete the old key, then *AddKey* to add the new key. If there is more than one index file, this procedure must be repeated for each file for which the key has changed. Finally, call *PutRec* to update the record in the data file.

Reuse of Deleted Data Records

Turbo Access will automatically reuse previously deleted data records before expanding a data file when new records are added. Turbo Access maintains a linked list of deleted data records. When a data record is deleted, its first two bytes form a pointer to the next deleted record. Minus one (-1) indicates that the record is the last record in the list. Since a zero pointer (two bytes of zero) never occurs, you may reserve the first two bytes of each data record, and set them to zero when you add a record to the file. This will enable you to distinguish used records from deleted records if you process the file without reference to an index (for example, when you reconstruct a corrupted index file).

Duplicate Keys

In some applications, there is no guarantee that key strings will be unique. For instance, in an index based upon last names, duplicate keys may occur. Turbo Access only allows duplicate keys if the *Status* parameter in the call to *MakeIndex* or *OpenIndex* is 1.

When Turbo Access adds duplicate keys to index files, equal keys are ordered by their record number (data references), so that key entries with low references appear first. Normally, this will correspond to the order in which the keys are entered, since new data records are usually added to the end of data files.

The search routines *FindKey* and *SearchKey* always locate the first key entry; that is, the key entry with the lowest data record number.

When you want to delete a key from an index file with duplicate keys, it is not sufficient simply to specify the key string, since this string may identify several entries. To select a specific entry, you must also specify the data record number. The *DeleteKey* procedure will delete the key entry only if the string and the data record number match the values found in the index file.

Numeric Keys

If your application program requires numeric key values, you must convert these numeric values to strings before passing them to Turbo Access. There are two ways to do this.

The simplest approach is to convert the numeric value to its ASCII string representation using the Turbo Pascal standard *Str* procedure (refer to the *Turbo Pascal Reference Manual: String Procedures*). If you use this method, the resulting strings must be right-justified (appear to the far right of the field). This is easily accomplished by specifying a field width in the call to *Str*. The main disadvantage to this method is that the key length must be set to the maximum number of digits that may occur as opposed to the number of bytes required to store the number in its binary format.

The second approach takes advantage of the compactness of integers in binary format. The routines shown here can be used to "pack" and "unpack" integers to and from strings. *IntToStr* converts an integer to a string, and *StrToInt* converts a string into an integer. The strings returned by *IntToStr* are two characters long; the strings passed to *StrToInt* must likewise be two characters long.

```
type
  string2=string[2];

function IntToStr (N : integer) : string2;
begin
  N := N + $8000;
  IntToStr := Chr(Hi(N)) + Chr(Lo(N));
end;


function StrToInt(S : string2): integer;
begin
  StrToInt := Swap(Ord(S[1])) + Ord(S[2]) + $8000;
end;
```

The previous routines operate on signed integers (-32768 to 32767). If the integers are to be interpreted as unsigned quantities, simply remove the additions of $8000.

Data File Splitting

A Turbo Access index file must be contained in a single disk file. Data files may, however, be spread over more than one disk file; the total number of records must not exceed 65,536. The splitting of a data file is quite simple to implement and best illustrated by an example.

Assume that each data file can hold 10,000 records and that we need to store up to 30,000 records; we will require three data file disks. When a record is added to the first file, the data record number is entered directly into the index file. However, when records are added to the second and third file, we add 10,000 or 20,000 to the record number. Later, when the index file is read, record numbers can be divided by 10,000 to determine in which files the records reside, and the remainders from the divisions are the actual data record numbers. Since the first record number in a data file is 1, you must subtract 1 before dividing and add 1 to the remainder to obtain the correct results.

Skeleton Program

A skeleton program that uses Turbo Access might look like this:

```
program YourProgram;

const
  MaxDataRecSize    = 132;   { Maximum record size          }
  MaxKeyLen         = 25;    { Maximum key length           }
  PageSize          = 24;    { 24 items per page            }
  Order             = 12;    { Half the PageSize            }
  PageStackSize     = 8;     { Page buffer size             }
  MaxHeight         = 5;     { Maximum B+tree Height        }

{$I ACCESS.BOX}   { Needed for Turbo Access programs        }
{$I ADDKEY.BOX}   { Needed to add entries to index files    }
{$I DELKEY.BOX}   { Needed to delete entries from index files}
{$I GETKEY.BOX}   { Needed to search the B+tree             }

type
  MyDataRec = Record
                DataStatus: integer;    {   2 bytes        }
                Field1    : string[50]; {  51 bytes        }
                Field2    : string[78]; {  79 bytes        }
              end;                       { 132 total bytes  }

var
  MyData : DataFile;
  MyIndx : IndexFile;


  { Any other variable and procedure declarations needed
    by your program.                                      }


begin
  InitIndex;          { Needed if index files are used      }

    { Here you could OpenFile or MakeFile for data files    }
    { and then OpenIndex or MakeIndex for index files       }

  CloseFile;
  CloseIndex;

                      { The rest of your main program       }
end.
```

Turbo Access Programming Examples

The examples in this section demonstrate some common operations on a sample customer database. We'll show you how to generate a database and accompanying index file, define records and keys, and access and update the database. The techniques used in this example are the same for more complex databases with larger records and several index and data files.

This example is contained on your distribution diskette under the file name TBDEMO.PAS. A more extensive and detailed example of a customer database program can be found in the files BTREE.PAS and BTREE.INC.

Defining the Record

Suppose you wish to create a customer database so you can easily find phone numbers and other pertinent information. The first thing you must do is decide what information you want to store about each customer. For example, let's say you need to store the following information:

> Customer name
> Company name
> Customer code
> Address
> Phone Number
> Other remarks

This list of information constitutes one data record. Each separate piece of information is one or more fields in the record. In a program, the record definition might look like this:

```
type
  CustRec = record
              CustStatus : integer;
              CustCode   : string[15];
              EntryDate  : string[8];
              FirstName  : string[15];
              LastName   : string[30];
              Company    : string[40];
              Addr1      : string[40];
              Addr2      : string[40];
              Phone      : string[15];
              PhoneExt   : string[5];
              Remarks1   : string[40];
              Remarks2   : string[40];
              Remarks3   : string[40];
            end;
```

The *CustStatus* field is included in most Toolbox database records to allow the program to distinguish between deleted and non-deleted records, since the *DeleteRec* procedure uses the first two bytes of a record for its own purposes. The remaining fields are derived from the list of information you wish to store.

Creating the Program

Now that we've decided on an appropriate data structure, we can build a program that will allow a user to input, access, update and delete the desired information. When designing the program, we should consider the appearance of the program to the user, since it will define the way a user can access and manipulate the data. A well-defined user interface helps determine which Toolbox routines we should include in the program, and which procedures we must write.

The first thing that appears on the screen should tell the user what options are available. A menu such as the following could be used to list the functions of the program.

1) List Customer Records
2) Find a Record by Customer Code
3) Search on Partial Customer Code
4) Next Customer
5) Previous Customer
6) Add to Customer Database
7) Update a Customer Record
8) Delete a Customer Record
9) Rebuild Index files
10) Exit

This menu tells the user what he or she can do with customer records, and that it is possible to rebuild an index file.

Before this menu can be displayed, the program must initialize files and global variables. Our main program might look like this:

```
begin
  InitIndex;
  Finished := False;
  OpenDataFile(CustFile,'CustFile.dat',SizeOf(CustRec));
  OpenIndexFile(CodeIndx,'CodeFile.Ndx',
                SizeOf(Customer.CustCode)-1,NoDuplicates);
  repeat
    case menu of
      '1','L': ListCustomers(CustFile);
      '2','F': FindCustomer(CustFile,CodeIndx);
      '3','S': SearchCustomer(CustFile,CodeIndx);
      '4','N': NextCustomer(CustFile,CodeIndx);
      '5','P': PreviousCustomer(CustFile,CodeIndx);
      '6','A': AddCustomer(CustFile,CodeIndx);
      '7','U': UpdateCustomer(CustFile,CodeIndx);
      '8','D': DeleteCustomer(CustFile,CodeIndx);
      '9','R': RebuildIndex(CustFile,CodeIndx);
      '0','E': Finished := True;
      else;
    end;
  until Finished;
  CloseIndex(CodeIndx);
  CloseFile(CustFile);
end.
```

First, the program calls a routine to open or, if necessary, create a file to hold the customer information. Next, an index file is opened so that a data record can be located by customer code. Once initialization is completed, the main program calls a procedure that displays a menu, then returns the user's menu selection. When the user is finished with the program, the index and data files are closed.

Note: Data and index files *must* be closed before terminating the program, or the files will not be recorded correctly on disk. After making any changes to these files, be sure that you close the file properly with the *CloseIndex* and *CloseFile* routines before you end the program.

Opening a Data File

To initialize the program, we use *OpenFile* to open an existing file and *MakeFile* to create a new data file. In the following example, these routines are combined into a procedure that opens the file if it exists. If the file does not exist, the procedure asks the user if the file should be created.

```
procedure OpenDataFile(var CustFile : DataFile;
                           Fname     : FilenameType;
                           Size      : integer    );
var
  create : char;
begin
  OpenFile(CustFile, fname, Size);
  if not OK then
  begin
    Writeln(' The data file: ',fname,' was not found.');
    Write('Do you wish to create it? ');
    Read(KBD,create); Writeln;
    if UpCase(create) = 'Y' then
      MakeFile(CustFile,fname,Size);
    else Stop;
  end;
  if not OK then Stop;
end; { OpenDataFile }
```

Both *MakeFile* and *OpenFile* take three arguments:

*   File variable of type *DataFile*
*   Name of the file
*   Size of the data record to be stored in the file

The *DataFile* type is declared in the Toolbox ACCESS.BOX module, and the variable *CustFile* must be declared in our program. The filename is a string following the operating system's normal file-naming conventions.

The *SizeOf* function is the best way to pass the last parameter, since it will always reflect the true record size at run time, even if the record definition changes; a static constant will not. To use the previous routine, pass the *DataFile* variable, the name of the disk file, and the size of the data record to be stored. The call from the main program looks like this:

```
OpenDataFile(CustFile,'CustFile.dat',SizeOf(CustRec));
```

After a call to *OpenDataFile*, either a data file is opened or the program has stopped. The global variable *OK* (declared in the AC-CESS.BOX module) reflects the result of the call to *OpenFile* or *MakeFile* and is checked for success or failure. If the *OpenFile* call fails, the user is asked if he or she wants to create the file. If the user decides not to create the file or if an error occurred during file creation, an error handling routine should be called. In the following example, the *Stop* procedure is a critical error handler that can be called from anywhere. *Stop* displays an error message and stops the program.

```
procedure Stop;
begin
  GotoXY(1,24);
  ClrEol;
  Writeln('Customer database program aborted.');
  Halt;
end;  { Stop execution }
```

Adding Records

After calling the *OpenDataFile* routine, our program can add records to the data file using the Toolbox *AddRec* procedure. *AddRec* takes three parameters.

- *DataFile* variable
- Variable to receive a record number
- Database record

The record number variable receives the location where the record was stored, and is used for building and updating index files (explained later in this tutorial). The last parameter is the record buffer which holds the information to be written to disk.

The following example illustrates how to construct a database and add records, with no index files. All that is required is a data input routine and the Toolbox *AddRec* procedure. The example assumes that *OpenDataFile* has already been called. The procedure repeats, requesting user input, then storing that information in the data file.

```
procedure BuildDataFile(var CustFile : DataFile);
var
  InputRec     : CustRec;
  RecordNumber : integer;
  Response     : char;


begin
  repeat
    InputInformation(InputRec);
    AddRec(CustFile, RecordNumber, InputRec);
    Write('Would you like to enter another record? ');
    Read(KBD,Response);
    Writeln(UpCase(Response));
  until UpCase(Response) <> 'Y';
end;
                    { BuildDataFile }
```

AddRec takes the information obtained from the input routine and appends it to the disk file represented by *CustFile*. The variable *RecordNumber* must be passed to *AddRec*. After the call is made, *RecordNumber* contains the physical location of the record that was written to the disk.

Although *BuildDataFile* is an effective routine, it is not very safe. This is because it ignores the fact that an index file is going to be used, and would allow us to enter two records with the same customer code. This would create a conflict when a customer code index file is created, since that would require that each customer have a unique customer code.

To solve this problem, we can incorporate the index routines when records are added (see the next section). Right now, let's look at one way to obtain user input.

We start by creating a simple data input routine:

```
procedure InputInformation(var Customer : CustRec);
begin
  Writeln(' Enter Customer Information ');
  Writeln;
  with Customer do
  begin
    CustStatus := 0;
    Write('Customer code: '); Readln(CustCode);
    Write('Entry date   : '); Readln(EntryDate);
    Write('First name   : '); Readln(CustCode);
{
       .

       .

       .                          }
    Write('Remarks : '); Readln(Remarks3);
  end;
end;            { InputInformation }
```

Although *InputInformation* does what it sets out to do, it is very simplistic, and is therefore error prone. For example, the standard Turbo Pascal *Readln* procedure allows as many as 128 characters to be entered. If fields are set up on the screen, a user could enter too many characters and disturb the display. Or, if one of the fields requires an integer and the user enters an alphabetic character and a carriage return, an I/O error would occur.

It is best to input data character-by-character, as suggested in Appendix A, "Tips for Toolbox Programmers." For a good example of a "safe" data input routine, refer to the *InputStr* procedure in the sample include file, BTREE.INC.

Note that the *CustStatus* field is set to zero. This marks the record as a valid, non-deleted record. In the next section, we shall see how to distinguish between deleted and non-deleted records in the database.

Creating an Index

Now that we have a data file and a way to input information, we can use an index file to build an efficient database. Index files are completely separate from data files. This means that, if you make a change to a data file, you must also make the corresponding change in the associated index file. In addition, an index file must be opened explicitly in much the same way as a data file.

The nice thing about index files is that they allow you to key a meaningful word or string to each record. In our example, a key could be the customer's name, the company's name or the customer's code. In some cases, each key will be unique, as when we assign a code number to each customer; in other cases, duplicate keys will be used, as when there is more than one customer with the same name.

All keys used by Database Toolbox routines must be strings. If you choose a numeric field (real or integer) as a key, you must convert it to a string before passing it to the index routines.

Since index information is stored in a separate file, we must use Toolbox routines to create the index file and then make entries into it based on our data file. Before calling any index procedures, we must call *InitIndex* to initialize the internal index structure. *MakeIndex* creates the index file, and *AddKey* associates a data record with a key.

We can take the same approach to opening the index file as we did with the data file; that is, we first try to open the index file, and if it does not exist, we create it. The following example shows a routine for opening index files:

```
procedure OpenIndexFile(var  CodeIndx : IndexFile;
                             Fname    : FilenameType;
                             KeySize,
                             Dups     : integer);
var
  create: char;
begin
  OpenIndex(CodeIndx,Fname,KeySize,Dups);
  if not OK then
  begin
    Writeln(' The index file: ',fname,' was not found.');
    Write('Do you wish to create it? '); <cr> Read(KBD,create);
    if UpCase(create) = 'Y' then
      RebuildIndex(CustFile,CodeIndx);
  end;
  if not OK then stop;
end;                        { OpenIndexFile }
```

The parameters passed to this routine are:

- Index file variable
- Name of the disk file
- Size of the key string to be used
- Value indicating if duplicate keys are allowed

These are the same parameters required by *OpenIndex* and *MakeIndex*.

The index file variable is of type *IndexFile* declared in the Database Toolbox ACCESS.BOX module. The file name is a standard string. Since the Toolbox routines must know the correct length of the key string, use (*SizeOf*(KeyString)-1) when calling *MakeIndex* or *OpenIndex* (-1 compensates for the first byte that holds the length of the string). For example:

```
OpenIndexFile(CodeIndexFile,'CUSTCODE.NDX',
SizeOf(Customer.CustCode)-1,NoDuplicates);
```

The Toolbox must know if the program allows duplicate keys. If duplicates are not allowed, the Toolbox will inform your program when it tries to enter a duplicate key. In the previous statement, *NoDuplicates* is a constant set to zero. If duplicate keys are to be allowed, a non-zero value is used.

Now let's look at how to use these subroutines to build an index file keyed on customer code at the same time we are building a data file. In the sample procedure *BuildDataFile*, customer information was obtained and then inserted into the data file. This is the logical place to also insert key information into an index file. The following example modifies *BuildDataFile* to make it into a general routine for adding customer records.

The major differences between the *AddCustomer* routine on the next page and *BuildDataFile* are that the extra statements, *AddKey* and *FindKey*, are added, and it is assumed that *OpenIndexFile* has been called. *AddCustomer* makes sure that every time a record is added to the database the index is also updated. In addition, it will not allow records with duplicate customer codes to be entered into either the index file or the data file.

```
procedure AddCustomer(var CustFile : DataFile;
                      var CodeIndx : IndexFile);
var
  RecordNumber    : integer;
  Response        : char;
  TempCode        : string[15];
begin
  repeat
    InputInformation(Customer);
    FindKey(CodeIndx,RecordNumber,TempCode);
    if not OK then
    begin
      AddRec(CustFile,RecordNumber,Customer);
      AddKey(CodeIndx,RecordNumber,Customer.CustCode);
      Write('Add another record? ');
    end
    else Write('Duplicate code exists. Try another code? ');
    Read(KBD,Response); Writeln
  until UpCase(Response) <> 'Y';
end;                              { Add a Customer }
```

After the information is input, *FindKey* is called to see if there is already a database entry with this key. If *FindKey* sets *OK* to TRUE, a duplicate key message is displayed onscreen; otherwise, the record is added to the data file. *AddRec* returns the location of the data record in the file, which is passed along with the key to the *AddKey* procedure.

Rebuilding Index Files

Sometimes an index file is corrupted or lost while the corresponding data file remains intact. This could occur if a program is stopped before it closes the files—usually if the machine is turned off, or if there is a power failure. In such cases, you need some way to rebuild the index files. A similar situation occurs when you decide to add a new index file to your database. For example, you may want a separate index keyed on customer name.

When building an index file from scratch, or rebuilding a corrupted index file, the general method is as follows:

- Step through the database record-by-record
- Extract the key information from non-deleted records
- Pass the key and the location of the data record to the *AddKey* procedure

This is why the *CustStatus* field was included in the earlier record definition, and why it was set to zero in the example *InputInformation* routine. As long as *CustStatus* is zero, the record is non-deleted. To use this feature in rebuilding index files, simply test this field before adding the key. For example:

```
if Customer.CustStatus = 0 then AddKey( . . .
```

In the previous example, *OpenIndexFile*, when the index file is created a call is made to *RebuildIndex*. This is done in case the data file is non-empty—for example, if the index file is missing but the data file contained valid data. *RebuildIndex* can also be called from the main program if the user suspects a corrupted index.

The following sample procedure overwrites the old code index file with a call to *MakeIndex*. It obtains the number of records in the data file with a call to *FileLen* (subtracting one to compensate for the system record). It thus steps through the entire data file looking for non-deleted records to add to the index file.

```
procedure RebuildIndex(var CustFile  : DataFile;
                       var CodeIndex : IndexFile );
var
  RecordNumber : integer;

begin
  MakeIndex(CodeIndex,'CodeFile.ndx',
          SizeOf(Customer.CustCode)-1,NoDuplicates);
  for RecordNumber := 1 to FileLen(CustFile) - 1 do
  begin
  GetRec(CustFile,RecordNumber,Customer);
  if Customer.CustStatus = 0 then
    AddKey(CodeIndex,RecordNumber,Customer.CustCode);
  end
end;                                          { Rebuild Index }
```

Each record in the data file is read into memory with the Toolbox *GetRec* function. Once in memory, the record can be checked to see if it is a valid non-deleted record.

Since we know the data file was created using the previous *AddCustomer* procedure, we know there are no duplicate keys in the data file. Upon completion, a new index file is created and the internal index structure is reset.

Access to the Data

Once the previous procedures have executed, you will have created a file that contains information about your customers and an index file keyed on customer code. Now what can you do with it?

You can access the data sequentially by using two Toolbox routines:

• *FileLen* to determine how many records you have

• *GetRec* to bring the records from disk into memory

For example, consider the following routine:

```
procedure ListCustomers(var CustFile : DataFile);
var
  NumberOfRecords,
  RecordNumber   : integer;
  Pause          : char;

begin
  NumberOfRecords := FileLen(CustFile);
  Writeln('                  Customers  '); Writeln;
  for RecordNumber := 1 to NumberOfRecords - 1 do
  begin
    GetRec(CustFile,RecordNumber,Customer);
    if Customer.CustStatus = 0 then DisplayCustomer(Customer);
  end;
  Writeln;
  Write(' Press any key to continue . . .');
  Read(KBD,pause); Writeln;
end;                                              { ListCustomers }
```

ListCustomers determines the number of records in the file with the *FileLen* function call. *FileLen* returns the number of records in the file (represented by *CustFile*) including the one system record and all deleted records. To look at every record in the database, we set up a **for** statement to loop (*NumberOfRecords* -1) times (-1 tells the program to ignore the system record).

Each iteration of the loop calls *GetRec* with the file variable, the record number, and a customer buffer to hold the information. Once the record is brought into memory, it can be processed like any other record structure in Pascal. Thus, a call to *DisplayCustomer* writes the appropriate fields from the customer record to the screen.

```
procedure DisplayCustomer(Customer: CustRec);
begin
  with Customer do
  begin
    Writeln;
    WriteLn('   Code: ',CustCode,'    Date: ',EntryDate);
    Writeln('   Name: ',FirstName,' ',LastName);
    WriteLn('Company: ',Company);
    Writeln('Address: ',Addr1);
    Writeln('         ',Addr2);
    Writeln('  Phone:',Phone,' ext. ',PhoneExt);
    WriteLn('Remarks: ',Remarks1);
    Writeln('         ',Remarks2);
    WriteLn('         ',Remarks3);
  end;
  Writeln;
end;                              { Display Customer }
```

A more sophisticated way to display information on the screen would be to locate each field with a *GotoXY* statement, use a *Write* statement (not *Writeln*), and then use the *ClrEol* statement to remove any other characters on the line. This is the method used by the BTREE.PAS customer database program; please refer to the *OutCust* procedure in the BTREE.INC include file for more details.

The previous example is useful for accessing every record in the database. However, it is not very effective for accessing one customer record, or for listing the customer database in sorted order by key. To be more efficient, we can create an index file keyed on a specific piece of information.

Indexed Access

Given an index file and a search key, the Toolbox *FindKey* procedure will search the index for a key that exactly matches the search key. If a match is found, the *OK* flag is set to TRUE, and the location of the data record in the data file is returned in the variable *RecordNumber.* If *OK* returns TRUE, the next step is to use *GetRec* to read the record into memory. If *OK* is set to FALSE, no exact match was found, and our program should write a message to the screen telling the user the record was not found.

The following sample procedure asks the user to enter a customer code as a search key. (A more sophisticated procedure would allow the user to edit or delete the record once it was found; for an example, see the *Find* procedure in the sample include file, BTREE.INC.)

```
procedure FindCustomer(var CustFile : DataFile;
                       var CodeIndx : IndexFile );
var
  RecordNumber : integer;
  SearchCode   : string[15];
  Pause        : char;

begin
  Write('Enter the Customer code: '); ReadLn(SearchCode);
  FindKey(CodeIndx,RecordNumber,SearchCode);
  if OK then
  begin
    GetRec(CustFile,RecordNumber,Customer);
    DisplayCustomer(Customer);
  end
  else Writeln('A record was not found for the key ',SearchCode);
  Write('Press any key to continue . . .');
  Read(KBD,Pause);
end;                                    { FindCustomer }
```

The Toolbox *SearchKey* procedure lets you search the database using only a partial key. *SearchKey* takes the same parameters as *FindKey,* but looks for any record with a key greater than or equal to the key being sought. Thus, *SearchKey* sets *OK* to TRUE if a key is found that is close to the key being sought. A procedure to implement a partial key search is almost identical to the previous *FindCustomer* procedure. Only the wording and the Toolbox call change:

```
procedure SearchCustomer(var CustFile : DataFile;
                         var CodeIndx : IndexFile);
var
  RecordNumber : integer;
  SearchCode   : string[15];
  Pause        : char;

begin
  Write('Enter the Partial Customer code: '); ReadLn(SearchCode);
  SearchKey(CodeIndx,RecordNumber,SearchCode);
  if OK then
  begin
    GetRec(CustFile,RecordNumber,Customer);
    DisplayCustomer(Customer);
```

```
    end
    else
    Writeln('A record was not found greater than the key ',SearchCode);
    Writeln('Press any key to continue  . . .');
    Read(KBD,Pause);
  end;                                    { SearchCustomer }
```

After a call to *SearchKey, FindKey, NextKey,* or *PrevKey,* Turbo Access remembers the last key that was accessed so that surrounding entries can be found. The Toolbox *PrevKey* procedure can be used to find the key before the last one accessed, and *NextKey* can be used to find the key following the last accessed. These routines are quite similar to *FindKey,* except that there is no need to prompt the user for a customer code, and the Toolbox call is changed to either *NextKey* or *PrevKey:*

```
procedure NextCustomer(var CustFile : DataFile;
                       var CodeIndx : IndexFile);
var
  RecordNumber : integer;
  SearchCode   : string[15];
  Pause        : char;
begin
  NextKey(CodeIndx,RecordNumber,SearchCode);
  if OK then
  begin
    GetRec(CustFile,RecordNumber,Customer);
    Write('The next customer is : ');
    DisplayCustomer(Customer);
  end
  else
    Writeln('The end of the database has been reached.');
    Writeln('Press any key to continue  . . .');
    Read(KBD,Pause);
  end;                          { Next Customer }
```

Now we can access any record in the customer database by code. The same technique could be applied to build other index files that could access customer records by other fields, such as name or company.

Note that the key field in the *FindKey* and *SearchKey* procedures is a variable parameter. (See page 20 of the Owner's Handbook for more discussion.)

Deleting Records

Deleting a customer record is quite similar to adding one. Rather than obtaining data from the sample *InputInformation* procedure, the user need only enter the customer code. For example:

```
Write(' Enter the Code of the customer to be deleted: ');
Readln(CustomerCode);
```

With this information, we can write a *DeleteCustomer* procedure. The procedure must delete the customer record from the data file and remove the appropriate key fields from any index files we are using. The following example prompts the user for a customer number, and then deletes it (if it exists) from the index file and the data file.

```
procedure DeleteCustomer(var CustFile : DataFile;
                         var CodeIndx : IndexFile);
var
  RecordNumber  : integer;
  Response      : char;
  CustomerCode  : string[15]; { Same as CustRec.CustCode field }
begin
  repeat
    Write(' Enter code of customer to be deleted: ');
    Readln(CustomerCode);
    FindKey(CodeIndx,RecordNumber,Customer.CustCode);
    if OK then
     begin
      DeleteKey(CodeIndx,RecordNumber,Customer.CustCode);
      DeleteRec(CustFile,RecordNumber);
      Write('Delete another record? ');
     end
    else
      Write('Customer code was not found. Try another code? ');
      Read(KBD,Response);
      Writeln(Response);
    until UpCase(Response) <> 'Y';
end;                              { Delete a Customer }
```

The *DeleteCustomer* procedure repeats, requesting a customer code to be deleted, and then trying to find the key in the index file. If the key is not found, it issues a "key not found" message. Otherwise, the key is deleted from the index file with the *DeleteKey* procedure. *DeleteKey* assigns the *RecordNumber* variable the location of the data in the datafile. This is then passed to the *DeleteRec* procedure, which marks the record as deleted.

Updating Records

Sometimes a customer may change his or her name or address. To effectively implement an update procedure, we need some way to display customer information in a record and allow the user to change it.

For simplicity, let's use the *DisplayCustomer* and *InputCustomer* procedures already developed. (We could also allow the user to edit each field in the data record without having to retype the fields that haven't changed. For an example of this technique, refer to the *InputStr, InputCust* and *Find* procedures in the example include file, BTREE.INC.)

The update algorithm first finds the record to be updated, then calls the procedure that changes the record. When editing is complete, the record is put back into the file by the Toolbox *PutRec* procedure. If any of the fields used for keys were changed during editing, the index files must be updated by deleting the old key entry and inserting the new key. This means that all key fields should be saved in temporary variables prior to editing. After the data record has been changed the key fields can be tested to see if the index files need to be updated.

The following sample procedure prompts for a code, displays the associated record, and allows you to re-enter it. The procedure then puts the record back in the data file and checks the key field to see if the index file needs to be changed.

```
procedure UpdateCustomer(var  CustFile : DataFile;
                         var  CodeIndx : IndexFile);
var
  RecordNumber   : integer;
  Response       : char;
  CustomerCode   : string[15]; { Same as CustRec.CustCode field }

begin
  repeat
    Write('Enter code of customer to be updated: ');
    Readln(CustomerCode);
    FindKey(CodeIndx,RecordNumber,CustomerCode);
    if OK then
    begin
```

```
        GetRec(CustFile,RecordNumber,Customer);
        DisplayCustomer(Customer);
        InputInformation(Customer);
        PutRec(CustFile,RecordNumber,Customer);
        if CustomerCode <> Customer.CustCode then
        begin
          DeleteKey(CodeIndx,RecordNumber,CustomerCode);
          AddKey(CodeIndx,RecordNumber,Customer.CustCode);
        end;
        Write('Update another record? ');
      end
      else
        Write('Customer code was not found. Try another code? ');
      Read(KBD,Response);
      Writeln(Response);
    until UpCase(Response) <> 'Y';
  end; { Update customer }
```

Note that the customer code is saved, and then later compared to the code field in the customer record input from *InputInformation*. If the two variables are not identical, the old key is removed from the index file and the new key is inserted.

Conclusions

By now, it should be clear that a simple database program can be quickly written and customized to a particular situation. The foregoing procedures demonstrate the bare-bones coding necessary to set up a working database. This code can be found on the disk in a file called TBDEMO.PAS. Many of the enhancements you might want to make to these procedures can be found in the more detailed sample program, BTREE.PAS.

BTREE.PAS—A Customer Database

The file BTREE.PAS on the distribution diskette is a complete source code listing for a sample customer database. You can use this database and tailor it to your own applications as you see fit. When you run BTREE.PAS, you will be presented with menus that will enable you to manipulate and maintain the database using Turbo Access. BTREE allows you to add, find, view, edit, delete and list customers of a predefined type (see the *CustRec* type definition that follows).

BTREE maintains three files:

- A data file (CUST.DAT)
- A customer code index (CUST.IXC)
- A name index (CUST.IXN)

The customer code index does not allow duplicate keys, whereas the name index does. When BTREE.PAS is run for the first time, it will automatically create an empty database.

The Main Menu offers three functions: *Update, List* and *Quit. Update* is used to add, find, view, edit and delete customers. *List* is used to list customers, and *Quit* is used to terminate the program.

On the Update menu, the *Add* function is used to add new customers. *Find* is used to locate a customer, either by customer code or by last (and first) name. To search for a specific customer code, simply enter it when the cursor moves to the customer code field. If it is found, the customer data is displayed and you may, if you wish, edit or delete it. To search for a name, enter an empty customer code. Then enter the last name and first name. Note that if a first name is specified, the first 15 characters of the last name must be entered in full. The scan will locate the first customer of the specified name or the first customer that follows the specified name if no exact match occurs. You can then use *Next* and *Previous* to move forwards and backwards in alphabetical order. Once you have located the desired customer, enter *Quit*. You can then edit or delete the record shown on the screen, or simply leave it unchanged.

List is used to list customers. Listings show the customer code, the name and the company. They may be output to the printer or to the screen, and they may be unsorted or sorted by customer code or name.

For further comments, read through the source code that follows.

Note: On systems with only 64K RAM, BTREE.PAS is too large to compile in memory. You should select the **C**ompiler option to generate a .COM file(.CMD for CP/M-86), and then compile BTREE to disk. To run the program, e**X**ecute from the Turbo Pascal main menu, or **Q**uit the compiler and run BTREE.COM.

```
BTREE.PAS / BTREE.INC Sample Source
***************************************************************


program DataBase;
{$A+,C-,R-,V-}



{ ***********************************************************}
{                                                           }
{               Turbo-access version 1.00                   }
{                                                           }
{                  DATABASE example                         }
{                                                           }
{               Copyright (C) 1984 by                       }
{                   BORLAND Int.                            }
{                                                           }
{ ***********************************************************}


const

    { data record Size definition }
    CustRecSize  = 342;                    { customer record Size }

    { Turbo-file constants }
    MaxDataRecSize = CustRecSize;       { max record Size    }
    MaxKeyLen      = 25;                { max key Size       }
    PageSize       = 16;                { page Size          }
    Order          = 8;                 { half page Size     }
    PageStackSize  = 5;                 { page buffer Size   }
    MaxHeight      = 5;                 { max B-tree height  }


var
    NoOfRecs     : integer;

{ include Turbo-file modules }

{$I ACCESS.BOX}
{$I GETKEY.BOX}
{$I ADDKEY.BOX}
{$I DELKEY.BOX}
```

```
type
  Str5    = string[5];
  Str10   = string[10];
  Str15   = string[15];
  Str25   = string[25];
  Str80   = string[80];
  AnyStr  = string[255];

{ character set type }
  CharSet = set of char;

{ customer record definition }

  CustRec = record
              CustStatus : integer;        {    CustStatus }
              CustCode   : string[15];     { customer code }
              EntryDate  : string[8];      {   entry date }
              FirstName  : string[15];     {   first name }
              LastName   : string[30];     {    last name }
              Company    : string[40];     {      company }
              Addr1      : string[40];     {    Address 1 }
              Addr2      : string[40];     {    Address 2 }
              Phone      : string[15];     { Phone number }
              PhoneExt   : string[5];      {    extension }
              Remarks1   : string[40];     {    remarks 1 }
              Remarks2   : string[40];     {    remarks 2 }
              Remarks3   : string[40];     {    remarks 3 }
            end;

var
  DatF          : DataFile;
  CodeIndexFile,
  NameIndexFile : IndexFile;
  Ch            : char;

function UpCaseStr(S : Str80) : Str80;
var
  P : integer;
begin
  for P := 1 to Length(S) do
    S[P] := UpCase(S[P]);
  UpCaseStr := S;
end;

{ ConstStr returns a string with
  N characters of value C }
```

```pascal
function ConstStr(C : char; N : integer) : Str80;
var
  S : string[80];
begin
  if N < 0 then
    N := 0;
  S[0] := Chr(N);                                          { define length of string }
  FillChar(S[1],N,C);
  ConstStr := S;
end;


{ Beep sounds the terminal bell or beeper }

procedure Beep;
begin
  Write(^G);
end;


procedure InputStr(var S     : AnyStr;        {   string to edit   }
                       L,X,Y : integer;       {   maximum length and
                                                  x,y coordinates}
                       Term  : CharSet;       { legal terminating
                                                  characters}
                   var TC    : char    );     { actual terminating
                                                  character}
const
  UnderScore = '_';
var
  P : integer;
  Ch : char;
begin
  GotoXY(X + 1,Y + 1); Write(S,ConstStr(UnderScore,L - Length(S)));
  P := 0;
  repeat
    GotoXY(X + P + 1,Y + 1); Read(KBD,Ch);
    case Ch of
      #32..#126 : if P < L then                { legal characters }
                    begin
                      if Length(S) = L then    { string full, remove
                                                  char from end }
                        Delete(S,L,1);
                      P := P + 1;
                      Insert(Ch,S,P);          { add new character }
                      Write(Copy(S,P,L));
                    end
```

```
                  else Beep;
  ^S          : if P > 0 then              { cursor left }
                   P := P - 1
                else Beep;
  ^D          : if P < Length(S) then      { cursor right }
                   P := P + 1
                else Beep;
  ^A          : P := 0;                    { beginning of string }
  ^F          : P := Length(S);            { beginning of string }
  ^G          :
                begin
                  Delete(S,P + 1,1);
                  Write(Copy(S,P + 1,L),UnderScore);
                end;
  ^H,#127     : if P > 0 then              { delete previous char }
                begin
                  Delete(S,P,1);
                  Write(^H,Copy(S,P,L),UnderScore);
                  P := P - 1;
                end
                else Beep;
  ^Y          : begin                      { delete entire string }
                  Write(ConstStr(UnderScore,Length(S) - P));
                  Delete(S,P + 1,L);
                end;
    else
     if
    end;  {of case}
  until Ch in Term;
  P := Length(S);
  GotoXY(X +  P +  1,Y + 1);                     { erase leftover underscore
                                                  characters }

  Write('' :L - P);
  TC := Ch;                                      { set terminating character
                                                  flag }

end;

procedure Select(    Prompt : Str80;
                     Term   : CharSet;
                 var TC     : char   );
var
  Ch : char;
```

```
begin
  GotoXY(1,23); Write(Prompt,'? ' ); ClrEol;
  repeat
    Read(KBD,Ch);
    TC := UpCase(Ch);
    if not (TC in Term) then
      Beep;
  until TC in Term;
  Write(Ch);
end;


{ ClearFrame clears the display frame, i.e. Lines 3 to 20 }
procedure ClearFrame;
var
  I : integer;
begin
  for I := 3 to 20 do
  begin
    GotoXY(1,I + 1); ClrEol ;
  end;
end;


{ OutForm displays the entry form on the screen }

procedure OutForm;
begin
  GotoXY(7,5); Write('Code :');
  GotoXY(29,5); Write('Date :');
  GotoXY(1,7); Write('First name :');
  GotoXY(29,7); Write('Last name :');
  GotoXY(4,9); Write('Company :');
  GotoXY(2,10); Write('Address 1 :');
  GotoXY(2,11); Write('Address 2 :');
  GotoXY(6,13); Write('Phone :');
  GotoXY(29,13); Write('Extension :');
  GotoXY(2,15); Write('Remarks 1 :');
  GotoXY(2,16); Write('Remarks 2 :');
  GotoXY(2,17); Write('Remarks 3 :');
end;

{ ClearForm clears all fields in the entry form }
```

```
procedure ClearForm;
begin
  GotoXY(13,5);  Write('' :15);
  GotoXY(35,5);  ClrEol;
  GotoXY(13,7);  Write('' :15);
  GotoXY(40,7);  ClrEol;
  GotoXY(13,9);  ClrEol;
  GotoXY(13,10); ClrEol;
  GotoXY(13,11); ClrEol;
  GotoXY(13,13); Write('' :15);
  GotoXY(40,13); ClrEol;
  GotoXY(13,15); ClrEol;
  GotoXY(13,16); ClrEol;
  GotoXY(13,17); ClrEol;
end;


procedure InputCust(var Cust : CustRec);
const
  Term : CharSet  =  [^E,^I,^M,^X,^Z];        { legal terminating characters:
                                                ^I = <TAB>
                                                ^M = <RETURN> }
var
  L : integer;
  TC : char;
begin
  L := 1;
  with Cust do
  repeat
    case L of
      1  : InputStr(CustCode,15,12,4,Term,TC);
      2  : InputStr(EntryDate,8,34,4,Term,TC);
      3  : InputStr(FirstName,15,12,6,Term,TC);
      4  : InputStr(LastName,30,39,6,Term,TC);
      5  : InputStr(Company,40,12,8,Term,TC);
      6  : InputStr(Addr1,30,12,9,Term,TC);
      7  : InputStr(Addr2,30,12,10,Term,TC);
      8  : InputStr(Phone,15,12,12,Term,TC);
      9  : InputStr(PhoneExt,5,39,12,Term,TC);
      10 : InputStr(Remarks1,40,12,14,Term,TC);
      11 : InputStr(Remarks2,40,12,15,Term,TC);
      12 : InputStr(Remarks3,40,12,16,Term,TC);
    end;
```

```
    if TC in [^I, ^M, ^X] then
    if L = 12 then L := 1
    else L := L + 1
    else
      if TC = ^E then
        if L = 1 then L := 12
        else L := L - 1;
  until (TC = ^M) and (L = 1) or (TC = ^Z);
end;


{ OutCust displays the customer data contained in Cust }

procedure OutCust(var Cust : CustRec);
begin
  with Cust do
  begin
    GotoXY(13,5); Write(CustCode,'' :15 - Length(CustCode));
    GotoXY(35,5); Write(EntryDate); ClrEol ;
    GotoXY(13,7); Write(FirstName,'' :15 - Length(FirstName));
    GotoXY(40,7); Write(LastName); ClrEol;
    GotoXY(13,9); Write(Company); ClrEol;
    GotoXY(13,10); Write(Addr1); ClrEol;
    GotoXY(13,11); Write(Addr2); ClrEol;
    GotoXY(13,13); Write(Phone,'' :15 - Length(Phone));
    GotoXY(40,13); Write(PhoneExt); ClrEol;
    GotoXY(13,15); Write(Remarks1); ClrEol;
    GotoXY(13,16); Write(Remarks2); ClrEol;
    GotoXY(13,17); Write(Remarks3); ClrEol;
  end;
end;


function KeyFromName(LastNm : Str15; FirstNm : Str10) : Str25;
const
  Blanks = '                ';
begin
  KeyFromName := UpCaseStr(LastNm) +
                 Copy(Blanks,1,15 - Length(LastNm)) +
                 UpCaseStr(FirstNm);
end;

{ Update is used to update the database }
```

```
procedure Update;
var
  Ch : char;

{  Add is used to add customers }

procedure Add;
var
  DataF : integer;
  Ccode : string[15];
  KeyN  : string[25];
  Cust  : CustRec;
begin
  with Cust do
  begin
    FillChar(Cust,SizeOf(Cust),0);
     repeat
      InputCust(Cust);
      Ccode := CustCode;
      FindKey(CodeIndexFile, DataF,Ccode);
      if OK then
      begin
        GotoXY(6,19);
        Write('ERROR : Duplicate customer code');
        Beep;
      end;
    until not OK;
    AddRec(DatF,DataF,Cust);                { add to data file  }
    AddKey(CodeIndexFile, DataF,CustCode); { add to index file }
    KeyN := KeyFromName(LastName,FirstName);
    AddKey(NameIndexFile, DataF,KeyN);      { add to index file }
    GotoXY(6,19); ClrEol;
  end;
end;

{  Find is used to find, edit and delete customers }
```

```pascal
procedure Find;
var
  D,L,I   : integer;
  Ch,
  TC      : char;
  Ccode,
  PCode,
  FirstNm : string[15];
  KeyN,
  PNm     : string[25];
  LastNm  : string[30];
  Cust    : CustRec;
begin
  if UsedRecs(DatF) > 0 then
  begin                                    { file empty? }
    Ccode := '';
    repeat
      InputStr(Ccode,15,12,4,[^M,^Z],TC);
      if Ccode <> '' then
      begin
        FindKey(CodeIndexFile,D,Ccode);
        if OK then
        begin
          GetRec(DatF,D,Cust);
          OutCust(Cust);
        end
        else
        begin
          GotoXY(6,19);
          Write('ERROR : Customer code not found'); Beep;
        end;
      end;
    until OK or (Ccode = '');
    GotoXY(6,19); ClrEol;
    if Ccode = '' then
    begin
      L := 1;
      FirstNm := '';
      LastNm := '';
      repeat
        case L of
          1 : InputStr(FirstNm,15,12,6,[^I,^M,^Z],TC);

          2 : InputStr(LastNm,30,39,6,[^I,^M,^Z],TC);
```

```
    end;
   if TC in [^I, ^M] then
    L := 3 - L;
  until (TC = ^M) and (L = 1) or (TC = ^Z);
  KeyN := KeyFromName(LastNm,FirstNm);
  SearchKey(NameIndexFile, D,KeyN);
  if not OK then
    PrevKey(NameIndexFile,D,KeyN);
  repeat
    GetRec(DatF,D,Cust);
    OutCust(Cust);
    Select('Find : N)ext, P)revious, Q)uit',['N','P','Q'],Ch);
    case Ch of
      'N' : repeat NextKey(NameIndexFile, D,KeyN) until OK;
      'P' : repeat PrevKey(NameIndexFile, D,KeyN) until OK;
    end;
  until Ch = 'Q';
end;
Select('Find : E)dit, D)elete, Q)uit',['E','D','Q'],Ch);
with Cust do
case Ch of
  'E' : begin
          PCode := CustCode;
          PNm := KeyFromName(LastName,FirstName);
          repeat
            InputCust(Cust);
            if CustCode = PCode then
              OK := false
            else
            begin
              Ccode := CustCode;
              FindKey(CodeIndexFile, I,Ccode);
              if OK then Beep;
            end;
          until not OK;
          PutRec(DatF,D,Cust);              { update data file }
          if CustCode <> PCode then         { key was edited; update
                                              index file }
```

```
              begin
                DeleteKey(CodeIndexFile, D,PCode);
                AddKey(CodeIndexFile, D,CustCode);
              end;
              KeyN := KeyFromName(LastName,FirstName);
              if KeyN <> PNm then
              begin
                DeleteKey(NameIndexFile, D,PNm);
                AddKey(NameIndexFile, D,KeyN);
              end;
            end;
        'D' : begin
                DeleteKey(CodeIndexFile,D,CustCode);
                KeyN := KeyFromName(LastName,FirstName);
                DeleteKey(NameIndexFile,D,KeyN);
                DeleteRec(DatF,D);
              end;
      end;
    end;
  end { of UsedRecs(DatF) > 0 .. }
  else Beep;
end;

begin {Update}
  OutForm;
  repeat
    Select('Update : A)dd, F)ind, Q)uit',['A','F','Q'],Ch);
    case Ch of
      'A' : Add;
      'F' : Find;
    end;
    if Ch <> 'Q' then
    begin
      GotoXY(60,2); Write(UsedRecs(DatF) :5);
      ClearForm;
    end;
  until Ch = 'Q';
end;

{ List is used to list customers }
```

```
procedure List;
label Escape;
var
  D,L,LD   : integer;
  Ch,CO,CS : char;
  Ccode    : string[15];
  KeyN     : string[25];
  Name     : string[35];
  Cust     : CustRec;

begin
  Select('Output device : P)rinter, S)creen',['P','S'],CO);
  Select('Sort by : C)ode, N)ame, U)nsorted',['C','N','U'],CS);
  GotoXY(1,23); Write('Press <Esc> to abort'); ClrEol;
  ClearKey(CodeIndexFile);
  ClearKey(NameIndexFile);
  D := 0;
  LD := FileLen(DatF) - 1;
  L := 3;
  repeat
    if KeyPressed then
    begin
      Read(KBD,Ch);
      if Ch = #27 then
        goto Escape;
    end;
    case CS of
      'C' : NextKey(CodeIndexFile,D,Ccode);
      'N' : NextKey(NameIndexFile,D,KeyN);
      'U' : begin
              OK := false;
              while (D < LD) and not OK do
              begin
                D := D + 1;
                GetRec(DatF,D,Cust);
                OK := Cust.CustStatus = 0;
              end;
            end;
    end;
    if OK then
      with Cust do
      begin
        if CS <> 'U' then
          GetRec(DatF,D,Cust);
        Name := LastName;
        if FirstName <> '' then
```

```
      Name := Name + ', ' + FirstName;
  if CO = 'P' then
  begin
    Write(Lst,CustCode,'' :16 - Length(CustCode));
    Write(Lst,Name,'' :36 - Length(Name));
    Writeln(Lst,Copy(Company,1,25));
  end
  else

  begin
    if L = 21 then
    begin
      GotoXY(1,23);
      Write('Press <RETURN> to continue');
      Write(' or <Esc> to abort');
      ClrEol;
      repeat
        Read(KBD,Ch)
      until (Ch = ^M) or (Ch = #27);
      if Ch = #27 then
        goto Escape;
      GotoXY(1,23);
      Write('Press <Esc> to abort'); ClrEol;
      ClearFrame;
      L := 3;
      end;
    GotoXY(1,L + 1); Write(CustCode);
    GotoXY(17,L + 1); Write(Name);
    GotoXY(53,L + 1); Write(Copy(Company,1,25));
    L := L + 1;
    end; { of with Cust do .. }
  end; { of if OK .. }
until not OK;
if CO = 'S' then
begin
  GotoXY(1,23); Write('Press <RETURN>'); ClrEol;
  repeat
    Read(KBD,Ch)
  until Ch = ^M;
end;
Escape :
end;
```

```
{ Main program }

begin
  ClrScr ;
  Writeln(ConstStr('-',79));
  Writeln('Turbo-file Customer Database');
  Writeln(ConstStr('-',79));
  GotoXY(1,22); Writeln(ConstStr('-',79));
  Writeln;
  Write(ConstStr('-',79)); GotoXY(1,4);
  InitIndex;
  OpenFile(DatF,'CUST.DAT',CustRecSize);
  if OK then
    OpenIndex(CodeIndexFile,'CUST.IXC',15,0);
  if OK then
    OpenIndex(NameIndexFile,'CUST.IXN',25,1);
  if not OK then
  begin
    Select('Data files missing. Create new files (Y/N)', ['Y','N'], Ch);
    if Ch = 'Y' then
    begin
      MakeFile(DatF,'CUST.DAT',CustRegSize);
      MakeIndex(CodeIndexFile,'CUST.IXC',15,0);
      MakeIndex(NameIndexFile,'CUST.IXN',25,1);
    end
    else
    begin
      ClrScr;
      Halt;
    end;
  end;
  GotoXY(60,2); Write(UsedRecs(DatF):5,' Records in use');
  repeat
    Select('Select : U)pdate, L)ist, Q)uit', ['U','L','Q'], Ch);
    case Ch of
      'U' : Update;
      'L' : List;
    end;
    if Ch <> 'Q' then ClearFrame;
  until UpCase(Ch) = 'Q';
  CloseFile(DatF);
  CloseIndex(CodeIndexFile) ;
  CloseIndex(NameIndexFile) ;
  ClrScr;
end.
```

Using Turbo Sort

Turbo Sort sorts any data quickly and efficiently, with a minimum of coding on your part. Using the *Quicksort* algorithm, Turbo Sort's virtual memory management ensures that you are not limited to sorting in memory; if your data requires more memory than is available for sorting, the disk will automatically be used as an extension of memory.

This part of the manual teaches you how to use Turbo Sort in your own Turbo Pascal programs. It provides all the information you need to sort single data items and to sort on multiple keys.

How Turbo Sort Works

Turbo Sort is a function of type *integer.* The Turbo Sort function is called with one parameter, as follows:

```
SortResult := TurboSort(ItemSize);
```

where *SortResult* is an *integer* variable and *ItemSize* is an *integer* expression giving the size (in bytes) of the data items to be sorted.

Turbo Sort divides its work into three phases:

- The input phase
- The sorting phase
- The output phase

Each phase is carried out by a routine that you must write, as described below.

In the input phase, Turbo Sort calls the procedure *Inp* (which you write). *Inp* usually consists of a **repeat** or **while** loop that passes objects to the sort routine. *Inp* can generate these objects or retrieve them from a disk file, the keyboard or some other device (see SORT1.PAS for an example). *Inp* is called only once. When it finishes, the sorting phase starts.

Since Turbo Sort knows nothing about the type of data being sorted, it relies on the *boolean* function *Less* (which you write) to determine which of two data items is the smaller. The *Less* function is called repeatedly during the sorting phase and, for this reason, you should make it as fast as possible. When sorting is finished, Turbo Sort enters the output phase.

In the output phase, Turbo Sort calls the procedure *OutP* (which you also must write). *OutP* does exactly the opposite of *Inp*: after receiving its input from Turbo Sort, it retrieves a stream of sorted objects and sends it to the screen, printer, data file, or wherever you specify. *OutP* gets the sorted data one item at a time, allowing you to do with it whatever you please; you can write it to a file, put it in memory for further processing, print it, and so forth. Like *Inp*, *OutP* gives you complete freedom in dealing with your data because it is a procedure of your own design. *OutP* is called only once, and when it finishes, Turbo Sort terminates.

When the Turbo Sort function terminates, it produces an integer value that indicates whether sorting went well or aborted with an error.

Data Item Size

The parameter passed to Turbo Sort is the size (in number of bytes) of the data item you want to sort. The Turbo Pascal standard function *SizeOf* will give you this information, as shown in the following example:

```
ItemSize := SizeOf(DataItem);
```

where *ItemSize* is an integer variable and *DataItem* is the variable you want to sort (or the type of that variable).

Use of Memory

Turbo Sort automatically allocates space (*MaxAvail* minus 2K bytes to ensure ample space on the stack for local variables and parameters) on the heap for sorting. If your *Inp*, *Less*, or *OutP* subprograms require heap space, you must allocate space for them *before* calling *TurboSort* by using the standard Turbo Pascal procedures *New* or *GetMem*.

The *minimum* size required for sorting is:

    3 * *ItemSize*

or

    3 * 128 bytes

whichever is larger. If less space is available, Turbo Sort aborts and returns the error value 3.

Turbo Sort will perform sorting entirely within memory if space allows. If there is insufficient space for internal sorting, Turbo Sort's virtual memory management treats the disk as an extension of memory.

Maximum Sort Size

Turbo Sort can handle up to 32,767 records (*MaxInt*). If more records are passed to the sort routine, Turbo Sort aborts with error code 9.

Turbo Sort Programming Examples

The following program examples show you how to use Turbo Sort to sort on single data items and on multiple keys. The examples build in complexity, so it's a good idea to make sure you understand the simpler examples before you move on to more advanced sorting applications.

Example 1: Sorting A Customer Database on a Single Key

The following program example is contained on the distribution diskette under the file name SORT1.PAS.

Suppose you have a file of customer names you want to sort. The following example shows how you might write a sample program that reads data from such a file, sorts it by customer number, and outputs the sorted objects to the screen.

The file CUSTOMER.DTA on the distribution diskette contains 100 records of the type defined below, and is used by the example for input.

Start your program as you would any other with the type definition and the variable declaration:

```
type
   NameString = string[25];
   CustRec = record
                Number: integer;
                Name:   NameString;
                Addr:   string[20];
                City:   string[12];
                State:  string[3];
                Zip:    string[5];
              end;
   CustFileType = file of CustRec;

var
   CustFile : CustFileType;
   Customer : CustRec;
   Results  : integer;

   {$I SORT.BOX}
```

CustRec is the data item to be read from the file, sorted and output to the screen.

The include statement, {$I SORT.BOX}, causes the compiler to include the file SORT.BOX during compilation. This file contains the *TurboSort* function and related declarations.

After making these declarations, you are ready to write the three simple subprograms *Inp, Less* and *OutP.* The following subsections explain each of these.

The Inp Procedure

Because the *Inp* procedure is called from the *TurboSort* function in the SORT.BOX file, it must be forward declared prior to the declaration of *TurboSort.* The SORT.BOX file contains the necessary declaration. Your *Inp* procedure should look like this:

```
procedure Inp;
{ This procedure is forward declared in SORT.BOX.  It sends a stream
  of records to the sort routine.
}
var
  rec : integer;   { counts the number of records read from data file  }
begin
  rec := 0;
  Writeln;
  Writeln('Input routine - sending ', FileSize(CustFile),
          ' records to sort:');
  repeat
    rec := rec + 1;          {incremental record count                }
    Write(#13, rec:6);       {display record count,  stay on  same line}
    Read(CustFile,Customer);
    SortRelease(Customer);   {send records to TurboSort until EOF      }
    until EOF(CustFile);
  Writeln;
  Writeln;
  Writeln('Done with input - sorting ',
          FileSize(CustFile), ' records . . .');
end; { Inp }
```

The *Inp* procedure is called only once from *TurboSort*. It first reads records from the data file *CustFile*, and then passes them on for sorting with calls to the procedure *SortRelease* (which is also included in the SORT.BOX file). This process is repeated until end-of-file is reached. The parameter to *SortRelease* is untyped, which means that you can pass data variables of any type to *SortRelease*.

You have now read all of your input data and passed it on for sorting.

The Less Function

Like *Inp*, the *Less* function is forward declared in the SORT.BOX file as a boolean function with two untyped parameters *X* and *Y*. The type and parameters must not be repeated in your declaration of *Less*, which should look like this:

```
function Less;
{ This boolean function is forward declared in SORT.BOX and has
  two parameters, X and Y.   Because this function is called so
  often,  the number of  statements in this  function should be
  kept to a minimum.
}
var
  FirstCust  : CustRec absolute X;
  SecondCust : CustRec absolute Y;
begin
  Less := FirstCust.Number < SecondCust.Number;  { define sort order }
end;  { Less }
```

The *Less* function receives two memory addresses in the parameters
X and *Y.* These are the addresses of the first byte of the first two data
items *TurboSort* is to compare. You then declare two variables "on
top" of these data items by declaring the variables as absolute at
addresses *X* and *Y.* The variables then contain the data items to be
compared.

In this example, the customer numbers are compared—i.e., a customer number is the sorting *key.* We could sort on the *Name*, the *Zip
code*, or any other field in the record, or even on multiple keys by
comparing more fields. But let's keep this example simple.

Less is called by *TurboSort* whenever two data items are to be
compared. When *TurboSort* has finished sorting, the output procedure *OutP* is called.

The OutP Procedure

Like *Inp*, the *OutP* procedure is called from the *TurboSort* function
and is therefore forward declared in the SORT.BOX file.

```
procedure OutP;
{ This procedure is forward declared in SORT.BOX.  It
  retrieves the sorted objects one-by-one.
}
var
  i : integer;
begin
  repeat
    if KeyPressed then Halt;   {  Key touched?  Stop  program}
    SortReturn(Customer);        {Display records, one per line}
    with Customer do
    begin
      Write(Number, ' ', Name,' ');          {Pad with spaces}
      for i := Length(Name) to 25 do Write(' ');
      Write(Addr);
      for i := Length(Addr) to 20 do Write(' ');
      Write(City);
      for i := Length(City) to 12 do Write(' ');
      Writeln(State,' ', Zip);
    end;                                     { with }
  until SortEOS; {Until all sorted objects have been retrieved}
end; (* OutP *)
```

The *OutP* procedure is called only once from *TurboSort*. It calls the *SortReturn* procedure, which is part of the SORT.BOX file. *SortReturn* returns one untyped data item in its parameter, which can then be output. The process is repeated until the *SortEOS* function (a boolean function in the SORT.BOX file) returns a value of TRUE.

The **with** Customer **do**... statement writes the sorted customer records to the screen, one record at a time, with each field left-justified. The output could instead be sent to a file, a printer or anywhere else you wish to direct it.

The Main Program

In your main program, you must first prepare the input file for reading with the Turbo Pascal *Assign* and *Reset* procedures. The sorting is then started with a call to the *TurboSort* function. In our example, this is done in an *Assign* statement, followed by a *WriteLn* statement which prints the value of the *TurboSort* function on the screen when sorting is over. This value tells you whether everything went well, or whether sorting was aborted with an error.

```
begin                                            { program body }
  OpenFile(CustFile, 'CUSTOMER.DTA');            { open data file to sort   }
  Results := TurboSort(SizeOf(CustRec));         { sort the file of records }
  DisplayResults(Results);                       { display sort results     }
end.
```

As described earlier, the parameter to *TurboSort* is an integer expression giving the size (in bytes) of the data item to be sorted. The standard function *SizeOf* is convenient to use because it returns the size (in bytes) of its argument.

Note: *SizeOf* takes a type or variable identifier as a parameter. For more information about *SizeOf*, see the *Turbo Pascal Reference Manual*.

Turbo Sort Termination

The value of the function *TurboSort* (printed by the sample program), indicates certain error conditions, as follows:

0   All went well.

3   Not enough memory available for sorting. The minimum size is three times the size of the data item to be sorted, or 3 * 128 bytes, whichever is larger.

8   Illegal item length. Item length must be > = 2.

9   More than *MaxInt* records input for sort.

10 Write error during sorting. This means either a bad disk or the disk is full.

11 Read error during sort. Probably due to a bad disk.

12 File creation error. The directory may be full, or you may be trying to access a non-existing directory (MS-DOS/PC-DOS v. 2).

Program Listing

The following complete example (described previously) is contained in the file SORT1.PAS on the distribution diskette.

```
{$C-}
program SortAFile;
{

  TURBO DATABASE TOOLBOX DEMONSTRATION PROGRAM:

  Demonstrates how to sort a file of records.

  Modified:  08/07/85

  This program takes the CUSTOMER.DTA file, sorts the records by
  the Number field, and displays the sorted records on the screen.
}

type
  NameString = string[25];
  CustRec = record
              Number: integer;
              Name:   NameString;
              Addr:   string[20];
              City:   string[12];
              State:  string[3];
              Zip:    string[5];
            end;
  CustFileType = file of CustRec;

var
  CustFile : CustFileType;
  Customer : CustRec;
  Results  : integer;

{$I SORT.BOX }
```

```
procedure OpenFile(var f : CustFileType; Name : NameString);
{ Display welcome screen, open data file }
begin
  ClrScr;
  Writeln('TURBO-SORT DEMONSTRATION PROGRAM');
  Writeln;
  Writeln('Opening data file');
  Assign(f, Name);
  {$I-}
  Reset(f);
  {$I+}
  if IOresult <> 0 then
  begin
    Writeln(^G, ' - Cannot find ', Name);
    Halt;                                                      { abort program }
  end;
end; (* OpenFile *)

procedure Inp;
{ This procedure is forward declared in SORT.BOX.  It sends a stream
  of records to the sort routine.
}
var
  rec : integer;                   { counts the number of records read from data file }
begin
  rec := 0;
  Writeln;
  Writeln('Input routine - sending ', FileSize(CustFile),
          ' records to sort:');
  repeat
    rec := rec + 1;                              {incremental record count}
    Write(#13, rec:6);                  {display record count, stay on same line}
    Read(CustFile,Customer);
    SortRelease(Customer);                  {send records to TurboSort until EOF}
  until EOF(CustFile);
  Writeln;
  Writeln;
  Writeln('Done with input - sorting ',
          FileSize(CustFile), ' records . . .');
end;                                                               { Inp }
```

```
function Less;
{ This boolean function is forward declared in SORT.BOX and has
  two parameters, X and Y.   Because this function is called so
  often,  the number of  statements in this  function should be
  kept to a minimum.
}
var
  FirstCust:  CustRec absolute X;
  SecondCust: CustRec absolute Y;
begin
  Less := FirstCust.Number < SecondCust.Number;
                                      { define sort order }
end;                                            { Less }



procedure OutP;
{ This procedure is forward declared in SORT.BOX.  It
  retrieves the sorted objects one-by-one.
}
var
  i : integer;
begin
  repeat
    if KeyPressed then Halt;    { Key touched?  Stop program }
    SortReturn(Customer);
    with Customer do
    begin
      Write(Number, ' ', Name,' ');
      for i := Length(Name) to 25 do Write(' ');
      Write(Addr);
      for i := Length(Addr) to 20 do Write(' ');
      Write(City);
      for i := Length(City) to 12 do Write(' ');
      Writeln(State,' ', Zip);
    end;                                { with }
  until SortEOS;                        { with }
end;                                    { OutP }
```

```
procedure DisplayResults(results : integer);
begin
  Writeln;
  Writeln;
  case Results of                                  { display sort results    }
     0 : Writeln('Done with sort and display.');
     3 : Writeln('Error:  not enough memory to sort');
     8 : Writeln('Error:  illegal item length.');
     9 : Writeln('Error:  can only sort ', MaxInt, ' records.');
    10 : Writeln('Error:  disk full or disk write error.');
    11 : Writeln('Error:  disk error during read.');
    12 : Writeln('Error:  directory full or invalid path name');
  end; (* case *)
end; (* DisplayResults *)

begin                                                      { program body }
  OpenFile(CustFile, 'CUSTOMER.DTA');              { open data file to sort   }
  Results := TurboSort(SizeOf(CustRec));           { sort the file of records }
  DisplayResults(Results);                         { display sort results     }
end.
```

Example 2: Advanced Sorting

The example in this section (SORT2.PAS on the distribution disk) shows you how to sort different kinds of data, and how to sort on multiple keys.

Sorting Different Data

We will use the one-key example from the previous section as a basis for a new program that can sort both the customer data we already know, as well as items in a stock list. The first thing we must do is add the definition of a new type to the program declaration, as follows:

```
type
  NameString = string[25];
  CustRec = record
              Number  : integer;
              Name    : NameString;
              Addr    : string[20];
              City    : string[12];
              State   : string[3];
              Zip     : string[5];
            end;
  ItemRec = record
              Number  : integer;
              Descrip : string[30];
              InStock : integer;
              Price   : real;
            end;
```

The new type *ItemRec* defines a data record that will hold information about items in the stock list. The file STOCK.DTA contains 100 records of this type, and is used by our program as input.

We also must declare new variables for the stock list file, and for the items in the stock list:

```
var
  CustFile  : file of CustRec;
  Customer  : CustRec;
  StockFile : file of ItemRec;
  Item      : ItemRec;
  Choice    : char;
  Results   : integer;


{$I SORT.BOX }
```

The *Choice* variable is used in the main body of the program to let us choose whether we want to sort the customer file or the stock file:

```
begin                                   { program body }
  FileOpen(Choice);                { open data file to sort   }
  case Choice of                   { sort the file of records }
    'C' : Results := TurboSort(SizeOf(CustRec));    { customer file }
    'S' : Results := TurboSort(SizeOf(ItemRec));    { stock file    }
  end;                                              { case }
  DisplayResults(Results);         { display sort results    }
end.
```

The program first prompts you to enter a *C* or an *S*, and then keeps reading the choice until one of these characters is entered. Note that the input is converted to uppercase, so your users can make their entries in either upper or lowercase.

Based on the choice the user makes, the **case** statement prepares the desired file for reading, calls *TurboSort*, and provides the size of the applicable data type as the parameter.

The *Inp* procedure also uses the variable *Choice* in a **case** statement to select the correct file for reading:

```
procedure Inp;
{ This procedure is forward declared in SORT.BOX.    It sends
  a stream of records to the sort routine.  It also keeps the
  user informed of how many records have been read.
}
var
  rec : integer;
begin
  rec := 0;
  Writeln;
  case Choice of
    'C': begin                                    {sort customer file}
          Writeln('Input routine - sending ', FileSize(CustFile),
                  ' records to sort:');
          repeat
            rec := rec + 1;                  {incremental record count}
            Write(#13, rec:6);      {display record count, stay on same line}
            Read(CustFile,C
            SortRelease(Customer);    {send  records to TurboSort until EOF}
          until EOF(CustFile);
          Writeln;
          Writeln;
          Writeln('Done with input - sorting ',
                  FileSize(CustFile),
                  ' records . . .', ^G);              { ring bell }
        end;                                           { C }
```

```
'S': begin                                          {sort stock file}
        Writeln('Input routine - sending ', FileSize(StockFile),
               ' records to sort:');
        repeat
           rec := rec + 1;                   {incremental record count}
           Write(#13, rec:6);   {display record count, stay on same line}
           Read(StockFile,Item);
           SortRelease(Item);        {send records to TurboSort until EOF}
        until EOF(StockFile);
        Writeln;
        Writeln;
        Writeln('Done with input - sorting ',
               FileSize(StockFile),
               ' records . . .', ^G);                { ring bell }
     end;                                            { S }
  end;                                               { case }
end;                                                 { Inp }
```

If the choice is *C* for customers, the customer file is read, and its data passed on for sorting; if the choice is *S* for stock list, the stock list file is read.

In the *Less* function, we must declare two new variables of **type** *Item-Rec.* Again, a **case** statement uses the variable *Choice* to determine which variables should be used in the comparison:

```
function Less;
{ This boolean function specifies sort priority.   It is
  forward declared in SORT.BOX and has two parameters,  X
  and  Y.    Record X is sorted "lower" than Y based on a
  comparison  between  the  fields specified below  (Name,
  Customer  number,  etc.).   Because  this  function  is
  called many times,   the number  of  statements in this
  function should be kept to a minimum.
}
var
  FirstCust:  CustRec absolute X; { customer file }
  SecondCust: CustRec absolute Y;
  FirstItem:  ItemRec absolute X; { stock file    }
  SecondItem: ItemRec absolute Y;
begin
  case Choice of          { define sort priority }
    'C': Less := FirstCust.Number < SecondCust.Number;
    'S': Less := FirstItem.Price < SecondItem.Price;
  end;
end; { Less }
```

As you can see, we use the field *Price* as the key for sorting the stock file.

The *OutP* procedure in this example is a little more elegant than the one in SORT1.PAS. It keeps the column headings at the top of the screen by deleting the topmost record each time it adds a new one. Run the program—a picture is worth a thousand words. Note that some terminals do not support line delete. If yours doesn't, substitute a single *Writeln* statement in the body of *Scroll*.

The **case** statement is again used in the last procedure, *OutP*:

```pascal
procedure OutP;
{ This procedure is forward declared in SORT.BOX.   It
  retrieves the sorted objects  one-by-one and displays
  them on the screen.  NOTE:  If your terminal does not
  provide  support  for  deleting a line,  you  should
  modify the Scroll procedure below.
}
var
  i, Line : integer;

procedure Scroll(Line : integer);
{ This procedure controls scrolling during output of records.
  If your terminal does not support line delete, substitute a
  single Writeln statement for the IF statement below.
}
begin
  if Line > 20 then
  begin
    GoToXY(1, 5);                        { first line below header    }
    DelLine;
    GoToXY(1, 24);                       { last line on screen        }
  end
  else GoToXY(1, Line + 4);
end; { Scroll }
```

```pascal
begin
  Write(^G);                              { ring bell - finished with sort!          }
  ClrEOS(5);                              { clear from line 5 to end of screen       }
  Line := 1;                              { initialize line count                    }
  case Choice of                          { retrieve records from sort & display     }
    'C' : begin
            repeat
              if KeyPressed then Halt;                    { Key touched? Stop program    }
              Scroll(Line);
              SortReturn(Customer);             { display the records, one per line     }
              with Customer do
              begin
                Write(Line:3, Number:6, ' ', Name,' ');
                for i := Length(Name) to 25 do Write(' ');  { pad with spaces     }
                Write(Addr);
                for i := Length(Addr) to 20 do Write(' ');
                Write(City);
                for i := Length(City) to 12 do Write(' ');
                Write(State,' ', Zip);
              end; { with }
              Line := Line + 1;
            until SortEOS;                   { until all sorted objects have been retrieved   }
          end; { C }
    'S' : begin
            repeat
              if KeyPressed then Halt;                    { Key touched? Stop program    }
              SortReturn(Item);                           { display the records, one per line    }
              Scroll(Line);
              with Item do
              begin
                Write(Line:13, Number:6, ' ', Descrip,' ');
                for i := Length(Descrip) to 30 do Write(' ');            {pad with spaces}
                Write(InStock:5, Price:8:2);
              end;
              Line := Line + 1;
            until SortEOS;           { until all sorted objects have been retrieved }
          end; { S }
  end; { case }
  Scroll(25);                               { make room for results message            }
  Scroll(25);
  Scroll(25);
end; { OutP }
```

If your input, output and comparison routines become more complicated, it's a good idea to isolate each in a separate subprogram, and then call these from the **case** statement, passing the necessary information as parameters.

Multiple Keys

Suppose you want to sort the stock data, not just on price as above, but on two keys: *primarily* on quantity in stock, and *secondarily* (if two items have the same amount in stock) on price.

This is easy to do. Simply rewrite the comparison of *FirstItem* and *SecondItem* as follows:

```
function Less;
var
  FirstCust:  CustRec absolute X;  { customer file }
  SecondCust: CustRec absolute Y;
  FirstItem:  ItemRec absolute X;  { stock file   }
  SecondItem: ItemRec absolute Y;
begin
  case Choice of             { define sort priority }
    'C': Less := FirstCust.Number < SecondCust.Number;
    'S': Less := (FirstItem.InStock < SecondItem.InStock) or
                 ((FirstItem.InStock = SecondItem.InStock) and
                  (FirstItem.Price < SecondItem.Price));
  end;
end;                                      { Less }
```

First compare the *InStock* fields. If one is larger than the other, this comparison determines which item is smaller; if they are equal, the next comparison—between the *Price* fields—determines which data item is smaller.

You could carry this scheme further, and sort on as many fields as you wish.

Program Listing

The following is a complete listing of the example described above, contained in the file SORT2.PAS on your distribution diskette.

```
{$C-}
program SortMultipleFiles;
{
TURBO DATABASE TOOLBOX DEMONSTRATION PROGRAM:

How to write a sort routine that can select which file of records
to sort.

Modified:  08/07/85

This program takes the CUSTOMER.DTA and the  STOCK.DTA files,  sorts
the one requested by the user and displays the sorted records on the
screen.
}

type
    NameString = string[25];
         CustRec = record
                 Number: integer;
                 Name:    NameString;
                 Addr:   string[20];
                 City:   string[12];
                 State:  string[3];
                 Zip:    string[5];
              end;
    ItemRec = record
                 Number:  integer;
                 Descrip: string[30];
                 InStock: integer;
                 Price:   real;
              end;

var
    CustFile  : file of CustRec;
    Customer  : CustRec;
    StockFile : file of ItemRec;
    Item      : ItemRec;
    Choice    : char;
    Results   : integer;

{$I SORT.BOX }
```

```
procedure ClrEOS(Y : byte);
{ Clear the screen from row Y to 24, then place cursor
  on column 1, row Y.
}
var i : integer;
begin
  for i := Y to 24 do
  begin
    GoToXY(1, i);
    ClrEOL;
  end;
  GoToXY(1, Y);
end; { ClrEOS }


procedure OpenFile(var Choice : char);
{ Set up screen, select which file to sort, open data file }


procedure Menu(var Choice : char);
{ Set up screen, select which file to sort. }
begin
  ClrScr;
  Writeln('TURBO-
SORT DEMONSTRATION PROGRAM':56);
  Writeln;
  Writeln;
  Writeln;
  Writeln('Turbo-
Sort is fast!   This program will ring the');
  Writeln('bell when the sort starts and then ring it again');
  Writeln('when the sort is finished.');
  Writeln;
  Writeln;
  Writeln('Sort');
  Writeln('—
');
  Writeln;
  Writeln('Customer file');
  Writeln('Stock File');
  Writeln;
  Write('Enter C or S: ');                    { sort customer or stock file }
  repeat
    Read(KBD, Choice);
    if Choice in [^C,  #27] then Halt;            { abort program if   }
                                                  { ESC or CTRL C is typed   }

    Choice := UpCase(Choice);
```

```
      until Choice in ['C','S'];
      ClrEOS(3);
      case Choice of                                    { draw column headings }
        'C' : begin
              Writeln('    No.  Company Name              Address',
                    '           City     State Zip');
              Writeln('—  — ——————  ',
                    '——————  ———  — ——');
              Writeln;
            end;              { C }
        'S' : begin
              Writeln(' ':10,
                    '   No.  Description               ',
                    ' Qty   Price');
              Writeln(' ':10,
                    '—  — ——————  ',
                    '— ——');
              Writeln;
            end;                                         { C }
      end;                                               { case }
    end;                                                 { Menu }

    begin                                                { OpenFiles }
      Menu(Choice);
      Writeln;
      Writeln('Opening data file');
      case Choice of
        'C': begin
              Assign(CustFile,'CUSTOMER.DTA');
              {$I-}
              Reset(CustFile);
            end;
        'S': begin
              Assign(StockFile,'STOCK.DTA');
              {$I-}
              Reset(StockFile);
            end;
      end;                                               {case}
      {$I+}
      if IOresult <> 0 then
      begin
        Writeln('  - Cannot find data file.');
```

```
      Halt;                                                    { abort program }
    end;
  end;                                                         { OpenFile }


procedure Inp;
{ This procedure is forward declared in SORT.BOX.   It sends
  a stream of records to the sort routine.  It also keeps the
  user informed of how many records have been read.
}
var
  rec  : integer;                    { counts the number of records read from data file      }
begin
  rec := 0;
  Writeln;
  case Choice of
    'C': begin
          Writeln('Input routine - sending ', FileSize(CustFile),
                  ' records to sort:');
          repeat
            rec := rec + 1;                        { incremental record  count        }
            Write(#13,  rec:6);            { display record count,  stay  on same line  }
            Read(CustFile,Customer);
            SortRelease(Customer);                 { send records to TurboSort until EOF      }
          until EOF(CustFile);
          Writeln;
          Writeln;
          Writeln('Done with input - sorting ',
                  FileSize(CustFile),
                  ' records . . .', ^G);                        { ring bell  }
        end;                                                    { C }
    'S': begin
          Writeln('Input routine - sending ', FileSize(StockFile),
                  ' records to sort:');
          repeat
            rec := rec + 1;                        {incremental record count}
            Write(#13,  rec:6);            {display record count, stay on same line}
            Read(StockFile,Item);
            SortRelease(Item);            {send  records  to  TurboSort until EOF}
          until EOF(StockFile);
          Writeln;
          Writeln;
          Writeln('Done with input - sorting ',
                  FileSize(StockFile),
                  ' records . . .', ^G);                        { ring bell  }
        end;                                                    { S }
  end;                                                          { case }
end;                                                            { Inp }
```

```
function Less;
{ This boolean function specifies sort priority.    It is
  forward declared in SORT.BOX and has two parameters,  X
  and  Y.    Record X is sorted "lower" than Y based on a
  comparison  between  the fields specified below  (Name,
  Customer  number,  etc.).    Because  this  function  is
  called many times,    the number  of  statements in this
  function should be kept to a minimum.
}
var
  FirstCust:  CustRec absolute X;                            { customer file      }
  SecondCust: CustRec absolute Y;
  FirstItem:  ItemRec absolute X;                            { stock file         }
  SecondItem: ItemRec absolute Y;
begin
  case Choice of                                             { define sort priority }
    'C': Less := FirstCust.Number < SecondCust.Number;
    'S': Less := (FirstItem.InStock < SecondItem.InStock) or
                 ((FirstItem.InStock = SecondItem.InStock) and
                  (FirstItem.Price < SecondItem.Price));
  end;
end; { Less }


procedure OutP;
{ This procedure is forward declared in SORT.BOX.    It
  retrieves the sorted objects  one-by-one and displays
  them on the screen.  NOTE: If your terminal does not
  provide  support  for  deleting a line,  you  should
  modify the Scroll procedure below.
}


var
  i, Line : integer;
```

```
procedure Scroll(Line : integer);
{ This procedure controls scrolling during output of records.
  If your terminal does not support line delete, substitute a
  single Writeln statement for the IF statement below.
}
begin
  if Line > 20 then
  begin
    GoToXY(1, 5);                              { delete first line below header }
    DelLine;
    GoToXY(1, 24);                                { add to 24th line on screen }
  end
  else
  begin
    GoToXY(1, Line + 4);                               { screen is not full yet }
  end;
end; { Scroll }


begin
  Write(^G);                          { ring bell - finished with sort!       }
  ClrEOS(5);                          { clear from line 5 to end of screen    }
  Line := 1;                          { initialize line count                 }
  case Choice of                      { retrieve records from sort & display  }
    'C' : begin
            repeat
              if KeyPressed then Halt;           { Key touched?  Stop program }
              Scroll(Line);
              SortReturn(Customer);          { display the records, one per line }
              with Customer do
              begin
                Write(Line:3, Number:6, ' ', Name,' ');
                for  i := Length(Name) to 25 do Write(' ');      {pad with spaces}
                Write(Addr);
                for i := Length(Addr) to 20 do Write(' ');
                Write(City);
                for i := Length(City) to 12 do Write(' ');
                Write(State,' ', Zip);
              end;                                                        { with }
              Line := Line + 1;
            until SortEOS;              {until all sorted objects have been retrieved}
          end;                                                            { C }
```

```
    'S' : begin
            repeat
               if KeyPressed then Halt;                    { Key touched?  Stop program }
               SortReturn(Item);                           {display the records, one per line}
               Scroll(Line);
               with Item do
                 begin
                 Write(Line:13, Number:6, ' ', Descrip,' ');
                 for i := Length(Descrip) to 30 do  Write(' ');   {pad with spaces}
                 Write(InStock:5, Price:8:2);
                 end;
               Line := Line + 1;
            until SortEOS;     {until all sorted objects have been retrieved}
            end;                                                            { S }
  end;                                                                  { case }
  Scroll(25);                                       { make room for results message }
  Scroll(25);
  Scroll(25);
end;                                                                  { OutP }


procedure DisplayResults(Results : integer);
begin
  case Results of                                     { display sort results }
     0 : Write('Done with sort and display.');
     3 : Write('Error:  not enough memory to sort');
     8 : Write('Error:  illegal item length.');
     9 : Write('Error:  can only sort ', MaxInt, ' records.');
    10 : Write('Error:  disk full or disk write error.');
    11 : Write('Error:  disk error during read.');
    12 : Write('Error:  directory full or invalid path name');
  end;                                                                { case }
end;                                                          { DisplayResults }


begin { program body }
  OpenFile(Choice);                                    { open data file to sort   }
  case Choice of                                       { sort the file of records }
    'C' : Results := TurboSort(SizeOf(CustRec));             { customer file }
    'S' : Results := TurboSort(SizeOf(ItemRec));             { stock file    }
  end;                                                              { case   }
  DisplayResults(Results);                          { display sort results    }
end.
```

Chapter 3
TECHNICAL REFERENCE

This chapter provides detailed information about all the files contained in the Turbo Database Toolbox. The first section gives an overview of the modular files you'll need to include in your application programs. The following section defines and describes the constants and types used by Turbo Access, the third section provides a quick reference guide to Turbo Access routines, and the final section describes all the Turbo Access functions and procedures.

Turbo Database Toolbox Files

The Turbo Database Toolbox is supplied on the distribution disk as an assortment of Turbo Pascal source files that you will need to "include" in your application program, using the { *$I filename* } include directive to the Turbo compiler. These files are organized as modules to allow you to choose only the files you need for compilation into your final program.

On your distribution diskette, all files for the Turbo Access and Turbo Sort systems have the extension .BOX. All sample programs have the extension .PAS or .INC.

Turbo Access Files

The following files belong to the Turbo Access system:

ACCESS.BOX   Basic data and index file setup and maintenance routines.

GETKEY.BOX   Search routines: *NextKey, PrevKey, FindKey and SearchKey.*

ADDKEY.BOX   The *AddKey* procedure used for inserting keys into index files.

DELKEY.BOX   The *DeleteKey* procedure used for deleting keys from index files.

TBDEMO.PAS	Turbo Access sample program
BTREE.PAS	Sample customer database
BTREE.INC	Include file for BTREE.PAS
SETCONST.PAS	Program to help determine correct access constants for your database programs.

The ACCESS.BOX module must always be included in a program that uses Turbo Access and it must always be the first module included. GETKEY.BOX, ADDKEY.BOX and DELKEY.BOX, however, may be included or omitted as required, and their order is of no importance. It is also possible to use the modules in program overlays.

Most Turbo Access routines return a status value by using a boolean variable called *OK*, which is automatically declared by Turbo Access. For example, the *OpenFile* procedure sets *OK* to TRUE if the file to be opened was found, and sets it to FALSE if it was not found. In case of severe or unrecoverable errors, a procedure called *TalOcheck* (in the ACCESS.BOX module) gains control. *TalOcheck* outputs the name of the file, the record number and the error code, and terminates the program.

Turbo Sort Files

The following files belong to the Turbo Sort system:

SORT.BOX	The *TurboSort* function and related procedures and functions.
SORT1.PAS	Sample Turbo Pascal program using Turbo Sort. Sorts data from the CUSTOMER.DTA file.
SORT2.PAS	Sample Turbo Pascal program using Turbo Sort. Sorts data from the CUSTOMER.DTA file on a single key and from the STOCK.DTA files on multiple keys.
CUSTOMER.DTA	Data for SORT1 and SORT2 above.
STOCK.DTA	Data for SORT2 above.

GINST Files

The following files belong to the GINST system:

GINST.COM   The GINST program. (.CMD in the CP/M-86 version)

GINST.COD   Object code for the generated installation program. Must be present when you run GINST.

GINST.MSG   Messages for GINST. These messages are also used to generate the .MSG file for your own installation program and must be present on the disk when you run GINST.

GINST.DTA   Terminal installation data, used for generating the .DTA file for your own installation program. May be omitted if you create an installation program for an IBM PC.

INSTALL.DOC   Documentation for the use of the installation program produced by GINST. You may include this text in your own manuals.

Turbo Access Constants, Types and Variables

The ACCESS.BOX module defines the following global types and variables:

DataFile   This type identifier is used to declare the data file variables. All Turbo Access data files are declared with this identifier, even though their data records are not of the same type and size.

IndexFile   This type identifier is used to declare index file variables.

OK   A boolean variable used to return the status of some Turbo Access routines.

The following sections define and describe, in alphabetical order, the constants used by the Turbo Access system; all constants are contained in the ACCESS.BOX module. Varying the values of these constants will vary search speed and the amount of RAM used by Turbo Access. As explained in Chapter 2, you can use the SETCONST.PAS program to help you set values for constants; the information given here is of a more technical nature, and assumes some understanding of B+tree structure. More information about B+trees can be found in Appendix B.

MaxDataRecSize

Declaration   const MaxDataRecSize = (an integer, 8...65,535, giving
                                        maximum data record size)

Purpose   *MaxDataRecSize* specifies the maximum record length, and should be set to the size (in bytes) of the largest data record your program will process. For example, if your program processes two data files with record sizes of 72 and 140 bytes, *MaxDataRecSize* should be set to 140.

Remarks   The surest way to determine the size of your data records is to write a small program to print out the *SizeOf* each data record. For example:

```
type
  MyRec = record
            Status: integer;
            Field1: string[40]; (Note: 41 bytes)
            Field2: string[80]; (Note: 81 bytes)
        end;
begin
  Writeln('The size of MyRec is ',SizeOf(MyRec));
end.
```

In this case, the number written is 124; the record size is 124 bytes. Use this technique with each data record your program will process to determine the *MaxDataRecSize*. When creating or opening a data file (using the *MakeFile* or *OpenFile* procedure), you can use *SizeOf(YourRecord)* as the parameter to the routines that need this information.

MaxKeyLen and *MaxDataRecSize* are set to the largest possible values for each type because the same internal structures are used to process each of the different index and data files. Thus, the internal structure must be large enough for the biggest key and record.

MaxHeight

Declaration   `const MaxHeight = (an integer, depends; see text);`

Purpose

MaxHeight determines the maximum height of the B+tree structure. This constant applies to all index files to be processed by your program. It does not affect the actual B+tree structure, but applies to each index file variable. *MaxHeight* is primarily used for sequential (forward and backward) searches of the B+tree. For calculation of *MaxHeight*, see below.

There are several equations that allow you to predict the size and efficiency of a particular B+tree; you can also estimate the disk space that will be used by an index file.

The maximum number of pages, *K*, to be searched to find a specific key in an index file with *E* keys is approximately:

$$K = \text{Log}(E) \, / \, \text{Log}(PageSize*0.5)$$

Thus, as *PageSize* gets larger, the number of searches (*K*) gets smaller. Large pages require fewer disk accesses, and therefore less time. The time required to perform a search within the page, once it has been read into memory, is of no significance compared to the time it takes to read the page from the disk.

The *MaxHeight* parameter required by AC-CESS.BOX corresponds to the integer part of *K* plus 1 (i.e., trunc(K) + 1). Therefore, when you have established the *PageSize* and the maximum number of data records in your database, compute *MaxHeight* as follows:

MaxHeight = Int(Log(E) / Log(PageSize*0.5)) + 1

Note that larger values of *MaxHeight* require very little extra memory (4 bytes for each increment of *MaxHeight*). It is therefore recommended that you add 2 or 3, instead of 1, to be on the safe side.

MaxKeyLen

Declaration	const MaxKeyLen = (an integer, 1...255);
Purpose	*MaxKeyLen* determines maximum key length. *MaxKeyLen* should be set to the largest maximum key length of the index file your program is going to process. For example, if your program will process three index files with maximum key lengths of 16, 10 and 25, *MaxKeyLen* should be set to 25. (Note that if a string is declared as **string**[25], its maximum length is 25 not 26, since we are concerned with length rather than size.)
Remarks	*MaxKeyLen* and *MaxDataRecSize* are set to the largest possible values for each type because the same internal structures are used to process each of the different index and data files. Thus, the internal structure must be large enough for the biggest key and record.

Order

Declaration	const Order = (an integer, 2...127 = *PageSize*/2);
Purpose	*Order* is half the value of *PageSize*, and represents the minimum number of items permissible on a B + tree page, except the root page (see Appendix B for information about page types).

PageSize

Declaration   `const PageSize = (an even integer, 4...254);`

Purpose

PageSize determines the maximum number of key entries allowed in each B+tree page. *PageSize* must be the same for all index files processed by your program, and must be an even number between 4 and 254.

Remarks

The number of bytes, *N*, occupied by each page in an index file is found as follows, where *KeySize* is the key length for the index file:

$$N = (KeySize + 5) * PageSize + 3$$

The maximum number of bytes, *D*, occupied by an index file is:

$$D = N * E / (PageSize*0.5)$$

where *E* is the number of index entries.

By combining the above two equations, it can be seen that the major determinant of index file size is the *KeySize*:

$$D = 2 * E * (KeySize + 5) + ((6 * E) / PageSize)$$

The above equation shows that an index file will be about (2 x *KeySize*) x the number of records that are indexed.

The previous two equations apply to a case in which all pages are only half full. In the average case, *PageSize* would have a multiplication factor of 0.75 (i.e., three-quarters full). This yields the following:

$$D = 1.5 * E * (KeySize + 5) + ((4 * E) / PageSize)$$

PageStackSize

Declaration   `const PageStackSize = (an integer, 3...254);`

Purpose

PageStackSize determines the page buffer size—the maximum number of B+tree pages that can be kept within memory at one time; the minimum number is three.

Remarks

In general, increasing *PageStackSize* speeds up the system, because the probability that a needed page will be in memory increases. Usually, *PageStackSize* should be between 16 and 32; however, your system resources may require other values.

The number of bytes, *M*, occupied in memory by the Turbo Access page buffer is:

M = ((MaxKeyLen + 5) * PageSize + 10) * PageStackSize

where *MaxKeyLen* is the largest key length used by the index file to be processed, and *PageStackSize* is the maximum number of pages that may be kept within memory at the same time (note that this must be at least three).

It is difficult to devise a general method for calculating the optimum values for *PageSize* and *PageStackSize*. *PageSize* usually lies between 16 and 32, depending on the maximum key size and the number of keys in the index. Smaller values will result in poor performance due to slow search times, and larger values will require too much memory for the page buffer stack.

The minimum reasonable value for *PageStackSize* is the value of *MaxHeight*. If *PageStackSize* is less than *MaxHeight*, the same page will need to be read several times to traverse the B + tree sequentially. In general, *PageStackSize* should be as large as possible (i.e., as memory resources permit). Specifically, if *PageStackSize* is much larger than *MaxHeight*, Turbo Access may store the root page and the entire first level of the B + tree within memory, thus reducing by at least one the disk accesses required to look up a key.

The values for *PageSize* and *PageStackSize* depend on the value of *E*, the total number of items in the tree. If there are *E* items in the tree, there will be *K* tree pages to be searched, where K = Log (E) / Log $(PageSize*0.5)$. For example, if *E* is equal to 100,000 and *PageSize* = 16, *K*=5. This means that, when searching, a maximum of 5 pages will be read into memory. During insertion, additional pages may be needed due to page splitting, and a value greater than *K* is needed.

The amount of free memory your system has is another factor in determining values for *PageSize* and *PageStackSize*. Since a page is approximately 550 bytes for a *PageSize* of 16, with a key string of 26 bytes, the page stack will take about 5600 bytes, if the *PageStackSize* is 10, i.e., (550 bytes per page + 10 bytes overhead) * 10 pages.

The Toolbox SETCONST program allows you to vary *PageSize* and *PageStackSize* to see the effects on memory usage and search efficiency. For more information, see page 13.

Quick Reference Guide to Turbo Access Routines

In the following list, Turbo Access routines are grouped by function into five categories: Data File Initialization, Data File Update, Index File Initialization, Index File Update, and Index File Search. The declaration for each routine is listed, followed by its page number in the look-up section that follows.

Data File Initialization

Data File Update

Index File Initialization

Index File Update

Index File Search

Procedures and Functions

This section defines and describes, in alphabetical order, all the procedures and functions contained in the Turbo Access part of the Database Toolbox. Sample usage for each procedure or function is given, followed by a detailed description of its function. Remarks, restrictions and examples are given where appropriate, as well as cross-referencing to related procedures and functions. The Turbo Database file that contains the procedure or function is given in brackets next to the name of the procedure or function.

AddKey [ADDKEY.BOX]

Declaration
```
procedure AddKey(var IndexF:IndexFile;
                 var DataRef:integer;
                 var Key            );
```

Usage   AddKey(IndexF,DataRef,Key);

Parameters   *IndexF* : index file to which key is to be added

DataRef : data record number to be associated with the key

Key   : key string

Function   *AddKey* adds a key string to an index file. *DataRef* is usually a data file record number returned by *Add-Rec*. On exit, the *OK* flag is set to TRUE if the key string was added successfully. *OK* returns FALSE if you try to add a duplicate key when such keys are not allowed (i.e., when the *Status* parameter in the call to *OpenIndex* or *MakeIndex* is 0).

Restrictions Since *Key* is an untyped parameter, you can pass string variables of any string type to *AddKey*. It is, however, up to you to ensure that the parameter is the correct string type; constants and string expressions are not allowed. If the *Key* parameter is longer than the maximum key length for *IndexF*, it will be truncated to the maximum length.

See Also   AddRec
             DeleteKey
             MakeIndex
             OpenIndex

Example   This code inserts the customer code string and the record number into the index file *CodeIndex*:
```
var
    CodeIndex    : IndexFile;
    RecordNumber : integer
    CustCodeStr  : string[40];
begin
     . { Code to open IndexFile and Add a Customer Record }
     .

     .
    AddKey(CodeIndex,RecordNumber,CustCodeStr);
end;
```

AddRec [ACCESS.BOX]

Declaration
```
procedure AddRec(var DatF :DataFile;
                 var DataRef :integer;
                 var Buffer      );
```

Usage   AddRec(DatF,DataRef,Buffer);

Parameters   *DatF*   : data file variable to which a record is
                          added

                DataRef : data record number

                Buffer : variable containing the data record to be
                          added

Function   *AddRec* adds a new record to a Turbo Access data
                file. This procedure returns the data record number
                of the newly allocated data record using the variable
                parameter *DataRef*. *DataRef* should be passed to the
                AddKey procedure when you enter a key value for
                the data record.

Remarks   Since *Buffer* is an untyped parameter, *AddRec* will
                accept any variable in its place. It is up to you to
                make sure that the variable passed is of the proper
                type.

                AddRec does not return a status value; it returns
                only if the data record is added to the file success-
                fully. If an I/O error occurs, *TalOcheck* will gain con-
                trol and terminate the program. We suggest that
                you call *FileLen* before calling *AddRec* to make sure
                that there is enough space on the disk.

                If any previously deleted records are available, they
                are automatically reused before the disk file is
                expanded.

Restrictions   *DatF* must be of type *DataFile*.

See Also   AddKey
                DeleteRec
                GetRec
                FileLen

This code stores *CustomerRecord* into file *CustomerFile*; and returns record location in *RecordNumber*.

```
var
  CustomerFile  : DataFile;
  RecordNumber  : integer;
  CustomerRecord : Record
                      Status  : integer;
                      Name    : string[80];
                      Address : string[80];
                      Company : string[50];
                   end;
begin
      .    {  code to open customer file and input  }
      .    {  information                           }
      .
  AddRec(CustomerFile,RecordNumber,CustomerRecord);
end;
```

ClearKey [*ACCESS.BOX*]

Declaration	**procedure** ClearKey(**var** IndexF:IndexFile);
Usage	ClearKey(IndexF);
Parameters	*IndexF* : index file that is prepared for sequential processing starting at the beginning or end
Function	*ClearKey* sets the index file pointer to the beginning or end of *IndexF.*
Remarks	Following a call to *ClearKey,* a call to *NextKey* will return the first entry in the index file, and a call to *PrevKey* will return the last entry in the index file.
	When Turbo Access index files are processed sequentially, a circular pattern is followed. When the index file pointer is at the end of the sequence, a request to read the next entry will return the first entry in the file. Likewise, when the index file pointer is at the beginning of the sequence, a request to read the preceding entry will return the last entry in the file.
Restrictions	None
See Also	NextKey PrevKey
Example	This code sets the search pointer to the first or last customer code in *CodeIndex*:

```
var
  CodeIndex : IndexFile;
begin
  {initialization code}
  ClearKey(CodeIndex);
end;
```

CloseFile [ACCESS.BOX]

Declaration   procedure CloseFile(**var** DatF:DataFile);

Usage   CloseFile(DatF);

Parameters   *DatF*: data file to be closed

Function   *CloseFile* closes a data file.

Remarks   If you make any changes to a data file, always call *CloseFile* for that file before terminating your program. Failure to do so may cause data to be lost.

It is good practice to close the file even if it has not been modified. This is required under certain implementations of Turbo Pascal (e.g., version 3.0 for MS-DOS or PC-DOS).

Restrictions   *DatF* must be of type *DataFile*.

See Also   MakeFile
OpenFile

Example   This code closes the customer data file, *CustomerFile*:

```
var
  CustomerFile : DataFile
begin
  { main program code }
  CloseFile(CustomerFile);
end;
```

CloseIndex [ACCESS.BOX]

Declaration	procedure CloseIndex(var IndexF:IndexFile);
Usage	CloseIndex(IndexF);
Parameters	*IndexF* : index file to be closed
Function	*CloseIndex* closes a Turbo Access index file.
Remarks	If you make any changes to an index file, always call *CloseIndex* for that file before terminating your program. Failure to do so may cause data to be lost or may corrupt the index file structure.
	It is good practice to close the file even if it has not been modified. This is required under certain implementations of Turbo Pascal (e.g., version 3.0 for MS-DOS or PC-DOS).
Restrictions	*IndexF* must be of type *IndexFile*.
See Also	OpenIndex
Example	This code closes the customer code index file, *CodeIndex*:

```
var
  CodeIndex : IndexFile;
begin
  { main program code }
  CloseIndex(CodeIndex);
end;
```

DeleteKey [DELKEY.BOX]

| Declaration | ```
procedure DeleteKey(var IndexF  : IndexFile;
                    var DataRef : integer  ;
                    var Key                );
``` |
Usage	DeleteKey(IndexF,DataRef,Key);
Parameters	*IndexF* : index file the key will be removed from
	DataRef : data record number associated with the key to be deleted
	Key : key to be deleted
Function	*DeleteKey* removes a key from a Turbo Access index file. On exit, *OK* is set to TRUE if the key was removed successfully. *OK* returns FALSE if the key was not found. If duplicate keys are allowed, *OK* will be FALSE if a matching data record number was not found, even though the key string existed.
Remarks	If duplicate keys are not allowed in the index file, *DataRef* need not be initialized. If duplicate keys are allowed, however, *DeleteKey* needs the data record to distinguish the keys from each other. To determine the data record number, you may, for example, use *SearchKey* in conjunction with *NextKey* and *PrevKey*. *DataRef* always returns the data record number of the deleted key.
Restrictions	The *Key* parameter must be a string variable. If it is longer than the maximum key length for *IndexF*, it will be truncated to the maximum length.
See Also	DeleteRec
	NextKey
	PrevKey
	SearchKey
```

Example   This code removes the customer code from the *CodeIndex* index file:

```
var
    CodeIndex    : IndexFile;
    RecordNumber : integer;
    CustCodeStr  : string[80];
begin
    { code to get key to be deleted             }
    DeleteKey(CodeIndex,RecordNumber,CustCodeStr);
    { possible code to delete record from data file }
end;
```

DeleteRec *[ACCESS.BOX]*

Declaration
```
procedure DeleteRec(var DatF:DataFile;
                        DataRef:integer);
```

Usage   DeleteRec(DatF,DataRef);

Parameters   *DatF*   : data file the record will be deleted from

                 DataRef : data record number

Function   *DeleteRec* removes a data record from a Turbo Access data file.

Remarks   The record number, *DataRef,* should be obtained from one of the following routines: *Deletekey, NextKey, PrevKey, SearchKey,* or *FindKey.*

The record is entered into the deleted data record list, so it may be reused by *AddRec* before the data file is expanded.

Restrictions   *DatF* must be of type *DataFile.*

Warning: Do not attempt to delete an already deleted record, or you may corrupt the linked list of deleted records.

See Also   AddRec
DeleteKey

Example   This code removes the customer record with number *RecordNumber* from the customer data file, *CustomerFile*:

```
var
  CustomerFile  :  DataFile;
  RecordNumber  :  integer;
  CodeFile      :  IndexFile;
  CustCodeStr   :  string[80];
begin
  DeleteKey(CodeFile,RecordNumber,CustCodeStr);
  DeleteRec(CustomerFile,RecordNumber);
end;
```

FileLen [ACCESS.BOX]

Declaration function FileLen(var DatF:DataFile):integer;

Usage FileLen(DatF);

Parameters *DatF*   : data file from which the number of records is found

Function *FileLen* returns the number of data records allocated to the data file given by *DatF.*

Remarks The length returned by *FileLen* includes the reserved record at the beginning of the file (record 0) as well as all deleted records.

Restrictions *DatF* must be of type *DataFile*

See Also UsedRecs, AddRec

Example This code sets *NumOfRecs* to the total number of records in the *CustomerFile*:

```
var
  CustomerFile   : DataFile;
  CustomerRecord : Record
                          Status : integer;
                          Name   : string;
                              .
                              .
                              .

                   end;
begin
  Write('The customer datafile contains ');
  Write(FileLen(CustomerFile)*SizeOf(CustomerRecord));
  Writeln(' bytes.');
end;
```

FindKey [GETKEY.BOX]

Declaration	procedure FindKey(var IndexF : IndexFile;
	                   var DataRef: integer;
	                   var Key);

Usage	FindKey(IndexF,DataRef,Key);
Parameters	*IndexF* : index file to be searched
	DataRef : data reference associated with found key
	Key : key string to search for
Function	*FindKey* returns the data record number associated with a key.
Remarks	*FindKey* locates the entry in the index file that exactly matches the string passed as the *Key* parameter. If the index file contains duplicate keys, *FindKey* always locates the first key.

On exit, *OK* is set to TRUE if a matching key is found. Otherwise, *OK* is set to FALSE.

The key field of *FindKey* is a variable parameter. If you search for a customer named *Smith* and the index is not found:

```
SearchKey(IndexF, DataRef, Name);
```

The global variable *OK* is set to FALSE and the value of *Name* is destroyed (it is actually set to the value of the last key read from the index file). Always use a scratch variable in your search routine if you don't want it changed.

For example:

```
Write('Enter name to find: ');
Read(Name);
Scratch := Name;    { Scratch is same type as Name }
SearchKey(IndexF, DataRef, Scratch);
if not OK then
   Writeln(' - Sorry:  I cannot find ', Name);
```

Restrictions	The *Key* parameter must be a string variable. If it is longer than the maximum key length for *IndexF,* it will be truncated to the *MaxKeyLen.*
See Also	NextKey PrevKey SearchKey
Example	This code sets *RecordNumber* to the record indexed by *CustCodeStr:*

```
var
   CodeIndex    : IndexFile;
   RecordNumber : integer;
   CustCodeStr  : string[80];
   CustRecord   : CustRecordType;
begin
with CustRecord do
   CustCodeStr := LastName + FirstName;
   FindKey(CodeIndex,RecordNumber,CustCodeStr);
   { code to process the date record accessed by record number }
   end;
```

GetRec [ACCESS.BOX]

Declaration

```
procedure GetRec(var DatF : DataFile;
                     DataRef:integer;
                 var Buffer      );
```

Usage

GetRec(DatF,DataRef,Buffer);

Parameters

DatF : data file the record is read from

DataRef : data record number

Buffer : variable to read the data into

Function

GetRec reads a specified data record into memory.

Remarks

Since *Buffer* is an untyped parameter, *GetRec* will accept any variable in its place. It is up to you to make sure that the variable passed is of the proper type.

Restrictions

Warning: *Buffer* is of a type smaller than the record size of *DatF*, other variables or code could be overwritten.

See Also

AddRec
DeleteRec
PutRec

Example

This code loads *CustomerRecord* with data from *CustomerFile*:

```
var
  CustomerFile   : DataFile;
  RecordNumber   : integer;
  CustomerRecord : Record
                     Status  : integer;
                     Name    :
                     Address : string[80];
                     Company : string[40];
begin
  { code to determine desired record number }
  GetRec(CustomerFile,RecordNumber,CustRec)
end;
```

InitIndex *[ACCESS.BOX]*

Declaration   procedure InitIndex;

Usage   InitIndex;

Function   *InitIndex* initializes the table used by Turbo Access index file routines.

Remarks   *InitIndex* must be called before other index file routines. Only one call is required, usually at the very beginning of the application program.

Restrictions *InitIndex* will corrupt index files if it is called when index files are open. It must only be called when there are no open index files and prior to calls made to *MakeIndex* or *OpenIndex*.

See Also   MakeIndex
OpenIndex

Example   This code sets internal structure of customer indexes:

```
var
  CodeIndex : IndexFile;
begin
  InitIndex;
  { code to open index files }
end;
```

MakeFile [ACCESS.BOX]

Declaration	```procedure MakeFile(var DatF : DataFile;```
	```FileN : string[14];```
	```RecLen : integer);```

Usage	*MakeFile*(DatF,FileN,RecLen);
Parameters	*DatF* : data file to be prepared for access
	FileN : string expression specifying the name of the new disk file
	RecLen : record length in bytes
Function	*MakeFile* creates a new data file and prepares it for processing.
	On exit, *OK* is TRUE if the file was successfully created. If *OK* is FALSE, there is not enough space on the disk or in the directory for a new file, or there is already a read-only file with that name.
Restrictions	*DatF* must be of type *DataFile*. *FileN* can be up to 14 characters long. The minimum record length for *RecLen* is 8 bytes. Use *SizeOf* (your record variable) when passing to the *RecLen* parameter.
See Also	CloseFile OpenFile
Example	This code creates a customer data file to store a record of type and size *CustomerRecord*:

```
var
   CustomerFile   : DataFile;
   CustomerRecord : CustRecType;
begin
   { code to determine if a new datafile should be created }
   MakeFile(CustomerFile,'CUSTFILE.DAT',SizeOf(CustomerRecord);
end;
```

MakeIndex [ACCESS.BOX]

Declaration
```
procedure MakeIndex(var IndexF      : IndexFile;
                        FileN       : string[14];
                        KeyLen,Status : integer);
```

Usage   MakeIndex(IndexF,FileN,KeyLen,Status);

Parameters   *IndexF* : index file to be prepared for access

            FileN   : string expression specifying the index file name

            KeyLen : maximum length of key strings to be stored in this file

            Status : 0 indicates that duplicate keys are not allowed; 1 means that duplicate keys are allowed

Function   *MakeIndex* creates a new index file and prepares it for processing. On exit, *OK* is set to TRUE if the file was created successfully. If *OK* is FALSE, there is no space on the disk for a new file, or the disc or file name is write-protected.

Restrictions   *IndexF* must be of type *IndexFile*. *FileN* may be up to 14 characters long. At the beginning of your program, a call must be made to *InitIndex* (once only) before calling *MakeIndex*.

See Also   CloseIndex
                 InitIndex
                 OpenIndex

Example   This code creates index file *CodeIndex* with no duplicates allowed, where *NoDuplicates* is a constant set to zero:

```
const
  NoDuplicates=0;
var
  CodeIndex  : IndexFile;
  CodeString : string[20];
begin
  MakeIndex(CodeIndex,'CODEFILE.NDX',SizeOf(CodeString)
  NoDuplicates);
end;
```

NextKey [GETKEY.BOX]

Declaration	```procedure NextKey(var IndexF : IndexFile;```
	``` var DataRef: integer;```
	``` var Key);```

Usage	NextKey(IndexF,DataRef,Key);
Parameters	*IndexF* : index file that has been prepared for sequential processing by a call to *FindKey*, *SearchKey*, or *ClearKey*
	DataRef : data reference associated with the key
	Key : key read from the next index entry
Function	*NextKey* returns the data reference associated with the next key in an index file. *NextKey* also returns the key value in the *Key* parameter.
	On exit, *OK* is set to TRUE unless no next index entry exists. In that case, *OK* is set to FALSE. When *OK* returns FALSE (that is, when the pointer is at the end of the index), *NextKey* returns the first entry in the index if it is called again.
Restrictions	Before the first call to *NextKey* for a given index file or after the index file is updated with *AddKey* or *DeleteKey*, one of the other index search functions (except *PrevKey*) must be called. The search functions establish the internal pointer used by *NextKey* and *PrevKey* for sequential processing.
See Also	AddKey ClearKey DeleteKey FindKey PrevKey SearchKey

Example   This code returns the record number and key of the next key in the search sequence:

```
var
  CodeIndex    : IndexFile;
  RecordNumber : integer;
  CustCodeStr  : string[20];
begin
  { code to set index pointer, i.e., ClearKey}
  NextKey(CodeIndex,RecordNumber,CustCodeStr);
end;
```

OpenFile [ACCESS.BOX]

Declaration
```
procedure OpenFile(var DatF  : DataFile;
                       FileN : string[14];
                       RecLen : integer);
```

Usage

OpenFile(DatF,FileN,RecLen);

Parameters

DatF   : data file to be prepared to access

FileN   : string expression specifying the name of an existing disk file

RecLen : record length in bytes

Function

OpenFile opens an existing data file and prepares it for processing by Turbo Access routines.

On exit, *OK* is TRUE if the file was found and opened successfully. Otherwise, *OK* is FALSE.

Restrictions

DatF must be of type *DataFile*. *File* may be up to 14 characters long. *RecLen* must be the same length as when the file was created.

See Also

CloseFile
MakeFile

Example

This code opens a customer data file to store a record of type and size *CustomerRecord*:

```
var
  CustomerFile   : DataFile;
  CustomerRecord : CustRecType;
begin
  OpenFile(CustomerFile,'CUSTFILE.DAT',SizeOf(CustomerRecord));
  if OK then {process the file}
end;
```

OpenIndex [ACCESS.BOX]

Declaration	```procedure OpenIndex(var IndexF : IndexFile;```
	``` FileN : string[14];```
	``` KeyLen : integer;```
	``` Status : integer);```

Usage
OpenIndex(IndexF,FileN,KeyLen,Status);

Parameters
IndexF : index file to be prepared for access

FileN : string expression specifying the disk file name

KeyLen : maximum length of key strings to be stored in this file

Status : 0 indicates that duplicate keys are not allowed; 1 means duplicate keys are allowed

Function
OpenIndex opens an existing index file and prepares it for processing.

On exit, the *OK* flag is set to TRUE if the file was created successfully. If *OK* is FALSE, there was no space on the disk for a new file.

Restrictions
IndexF must be of type *IndexFile*. *FileN* may be up to 14 characters long. At the beginning of your program, a call must be made to *InitIndex* (once only) before calling *OpenIndex*.

See Also
CloseIndex
InitIndex
MakeIndex

Example   This code opens index file *CodeIndex* with no duplicates allowed, where *NoDuplicates* is a constant set to zero:

```
const
  NoDuplicates=0;
var
  CodeIndex  : IndexFile;
  CodeString : string[80];
begin
  OpenIndex(CodeIndex,'CODEFILE.NDX',SizeOf(CodeString)
  NoDuplicates);
end;
```

PrevKey [*GETKEY.BOX*]

Declaration	procedure PrevKey(**var** IndexF : IndexFile;
	      var DataRef: integer;
	      var Key);

Usage	PrevKey(IndexF,DataRef,Key);
Parameters	*IndexF* : index file that has been prepared for sequential processing by a call to *FindKey*, *SearchKey* or *ClearKey*
	DataRef : returns the data reference associated with the key
	Key : returns the key from the preceding index entry
Function	*PrevKey* returns the data reference associated with the preceding entry in an index file. *PrevKey* also returns the key value in the *Key* parameter.
Restrictions	On exit, *OK* is set to TRUE unless no preceding index entry exists. In that case, *OK* is set to FALSE. When *OK* returns FALSE (that is, when the pointer is at the beginning of the index), *PrevKey* returns the last entry in the index if it is called again.
	Before the first call to *PrevKey* for a given index file or after the index file is updated with *AddKey* or *DeleteKey*, one of the other index search functions (except *NextKey*) must be called. The search functions establish the internal pointer used by *NextKey* and *PrevKey* for sequential processing.
See Also	ClearKey FindKey NextKey SearchKey

Example	This code returns the record number and key of the previous key in the search sequence:

```
var
  CodeIndex    : IndexFile;
  RecordNumber : integer;
  CustCodeStr  : string[20];
begin
  { code to set index pointer, i.e., ClearKey }
  PrevKey(CodeIndex,RecordNumber,CustCodeStr);
end;
```

PutRec [ACCESS.BOX]

Declaration	```procedure PutRec(var DatF : DataFile;```
	``` DataRef : integer;```
	``` var Buffer);```

Usage PutRec(DatF,DataRef,Buffer);

Parameters *DatF*   : data file to which record is written

DataRef : data record number

Buffer   : variable data is written from

Function *PutRec* writes a data record to a specified position in a data file.

Remarks Since *Buffer* is an untyped parameter, *PutRec* will accept any variable in its place. It is up to you to make sure that the variable passed is of the proper type. Buffer 3 is passed as a variable parameter to save memory.

Restrictions *DatF* must be of type *DataFile*

See Also AddRec
DeleteRec
GetRec

Example This code writes the *CustomerRecord* to the specified location in the *CustomerFile*:

```
var
  CustomerFile   : DataFile;
  RecordNumber   : integer;
  CustomerRecord : CustRectype;
begin
  { code to get and modify a data record }
  PutRec(CustomerFile,RecordNumber,CustomerRecord);
end;
```

SearchKey [GETKEY.BOX]

Declaration	procedure SearchKey(**var** IndexF : IndexFile;
	                var DataRef: integer;
	                var Key);

Usage	SearchKey(IndexF,DataRef,Key);
Parameters	*IndexF* : index file in which to search
	DataRef : data reference associated with found key
	Key : key string to search for
Function	*SearchKey* returns the data record number associated with the first entry in an index file that is equal to or greater than a specific key value.
	OK is always set to TRUE on exit, unless no keys are greater than or equal to the search key. In that case, *OK* is set to FALSE.
Remarks	*SearchKey* can be used to locate an entry in an index file when only the first part of the key value is known. If the index file contains duplicate keys, *SearchKey* always locates the first key.
	The key field of *SearchKey* is a variable parameter. If you search for a customer named *Smith* and the key is not found:
	`SearchKey(IndexF, DataRef, Name);`
	The global variable *OK* is set to FALSE and the value of *Name* is destroyed (it is actually set to the value of the last key read from the index file). Always use a scratch variable (or parameter) in your search routine if you don't want the variable changed.

For example:

```
Write('Enter name to find: ');
Read(Name);
Scratch  := Name;    { Scratch is same type as Name }
SearchKey(IndexF, DataRef, Scratch);
if not OK then
  Writeln(' - Sorry:  I cannot find ', Name);
```

Restrictions

Key must be a string variable. If it is longer than the maximum key length for *IndexF,* it will be truncated to the maximum length.

See Also

AddKey
ClearKey
DeleteKey
FindKey
NextKey
PrevKey

Example

This code returns the record number of the customer whose code is greater than or equal to the customer code:

```
var
  CodeIndex    : IndexFile;
  RecordNumber : integer;
  CodeString   : string[20];
begin
  { code to get search string }
  SearchKey(CodeIndex,RecordNumber,CodeString);
end;
```

UsedRecs [ACCESS.BOX]

Declaration   function UsedRecs(var DatF:DataFile):integer;

Usage   UsedRecs(DatF);

Parameters   *DatF*   : data file from which the number of
                              records is found

Function   *UsedRecs* returns the number of records in *DatF* that
                   contain valid data.

Remarks   In contrast to *FileLen*, this function does not include
                   reserved and deleted records.

Restrictions   None

See Also   AddRec
                   DeleteRec
                   FileLen
                   GetRec
                   PutRec

Example
```
var
   CustomerFile  : DataFile;
begin
   { code to initialize data file }
   Write('There are ');
   Write(UsedRecs(CustomerFile):1);
   Writeln(' in the database');
end;
```

Chapter 4
GINST—General Installation System

This chapter explains how to use the GINST (General Installation) program to generate installation routines for your Turbo Pascal programs.

How GINST Works

GINST creates installation programs that allow your customers to install your programs for their particular terminal(s). You may freely distribute the generated installation programs with any program you develop with Turbo Pascal.

GINST is not an installation program in itself; it is a program that *generates* installation programs, which will then install Turbo Pascal programs. GINST lets you create your application program on the computer of your choice, without worrying about where it's going to wind up after you've sold it to your end users. As long as you and your customers use the same operating system, and as long as their computers run Turbo Pascal, GINST will make sure your program gets up and running on the target system.

There are four operating systems under which you can run Turbo Pascal: MS-DOS, PC-DOS, CP/M-86, and CP/M-80. There are only three GINST installation programs, since the MS-DOS and PC-DOS versions are identical. The GINST-generated installation program can tell if the program it is installing was compiled for MS-DOS or PC-DOS and acts accordingly. However, GINST cannot convert a Turbo Pascal program compiled by PC-DOS to run under generic MS-DOS and vice versa.

When you load GINST, it first asks you to enter the name of the program to be installed:

```
-------------------------------------------
                  Turbo Pascal
          Installation Program Generator

       Copyright (C) 1984 by Borland International
-------------------------------------------

      Enter name of program to install: MYPROG
```

You can enter any legal file name—for example, MYPROG. If you don't enter an extension, COM is assumed (or CMD in the CP/M-86 version).

Next, you must enter the *first* (up to eight characters) name you want to use for the generated installation program files:

```
Enter first name for installation files: MYINST
```

As an example, let's run the installation program for the Turbo Pascal program MYPROG to produce the installation program MYINST. GINST produces the following message:

```
Creating MYINST.COM
Creating MYINST.MSG
Creating MYINST.DTA

Installation program for MYPROG.COM created
```

That's all there is to generating an installation program. When your end users run the installation program MYINST, they will be presented with a menu asking them to choose their terminal (or monitor, in the case of the IBM PC) from a list GINST provides; GINST will then put in the correct terminal control sequences for your application program.

Refer to the *Turbo Pascal Reference Manual: Installation* for an explanation of how to install your program; the procedure is identical to installing Turbo Pascal itself. A text file called INSTALL.DOC is included on your distribution disk and contains installation documentation that you may distribute to users of your program.

Note: As a condition under which you purchased the Turbo Database Toolbox, you may copy or paraphrase *only* the "Installation" section of the *Turbo Pascal Reference Manual* and include this information in your own documentation for your Turbo Pascal programs. Any other reproduction of the *Turbo Pascal Reference Manual* is a violation of the Borland license agreement.

Appendix A
TIPS FOR TOOLBOX PROGRAMMERS

The information in this appendix will help you design your Turbo Access programs. The general guidelines given here apply to *any* Toolbox program you write, regardless of complexity.

The Fundamentals of Program Design

Before performing the "real work" of database management, a good database program must control keyboard input as well as output to the screen, printer and disk drives. You should structure your program in a way that makes it easier to manage all these tasks: organize these "housekeeping" routines into modules and then put them in separate *include* files. Your main program will then look something like a table of contents. For example:

```
program DataBaseSystem;                              { Revised:  07/25/85 by Ace Coder }
{ This  program is a sample database system.

   Hardware requirements: 64K RAM

   Operating  System:    Any  PC-DOS,  MS-DOS,  CP/M-80  or
                         CP/M-86  machine that can run Turbo
                         Pascal.

   Data files used:  CUST.DTA, TX.DTA
   Index files used: CUST.NDX, ZIP.NDX, TX.NDX,
}

{$I CONSTANTS.INC }             { ACCESS constants  }
{$I DECLARE.INC  }             { other declarations }

{$I ACCESS.BOX   }             { ACCESS routines   }
{$I ADDKEY.BOX   }             { ACCESS routines   }
{$I GETKEY.BOX   }             { ACCESS routines   }
{$I DELKEY.BOX   }             { ACCESS routines   }

{$I INPUT.INC    }             { input routines    }
{$I ERROR.INC    }             { error handling    }
```

```
{$I FILES.INC   }                { open, close system }
{$I MAINT.INC   }                { entry & edit       }
{$I REPORTS.INC }                { print reports      }
{$I MENU.INC    }                { main menu          }

begin                                                      {   program body   }
  OpenSystem;
  Menu;
  CloseSystem;
end.
```

Each of the include files in this sample program is described in the following sections.

CONSTANTS.INC

You should be very methodical when you specify the values for Turbo Access constants, since they determine how efficiently your program uses memory. When set correctly, the constants *MaxKeyLen* and *MaxDataRecSize* optimize search and access speeds and help your program conserve memory. Incorrect constant values could lead to mysterious bugs and program crashes. Use the SETCONST.PAS program (on the distribution disk) to determine the best declarations for your application; see page 13 for an example of SETCONST.PAS.

DECLARE.INC

Put your type declarations in a separate module, then write a small program that includes this module and displays the size of the keys and records that will be stored and retrieved by Turbo Access routines. Given the following definitions in DECLARE.INC:

```
type
  CustName = string[25];                         { key for CUST.NDX file }
  CustZip  = string[9];                          { key for  ZIP.NDX file }
  CustRec  = record
    Name   : CustName;

      .
      .
    ZipCode : CustZip;
  end;                                            { customer record }
  TxRec = record

      .
      .
  end;                                            { transaction record }
```

your *SizeOf* utility program will look something like this:

```
program DetermineConstantSizes;

  {$I DECLARE.INC      include database declarations }

  begin                                                    { program body }
    Writeln('Largest = MaxKeyLen');
    Writeln('----------');
    Writeln('Customer name key: ', SizeOf(CustName)-1);
    Writeln('Zip code key:      ', SizeOf(CustZip)-1);
    Writeln;
    Writeln('Largest = MaxDataRecSize');
    Writeln('----------');
    Writeln('Customer record:   ', SizeOf(CustRec));
    Writeln('Transaction record: ', SizeOf(TxRec));
  end.
```

The length of the longest key is the value you should use for *Max-KeyLen*. Similarly, set *MaxDataRecSize* to the size of the largest record. Then determine the maximum number of records and keys that your program will be likely to use. Finally, using the SET-CONST.PAS program, plug in the above values and compute the optimum values for your data structures. As in any well-structured program, use constants, avoid global variables and pass parameters to procedures whenever possible.

ACCESS.BOX, ADDKEY.BOX, GETKEY.BOX, DELKEY.BOX

A good database program should have only one procedure that reads, one that writes and one that deletes records from disk files. The ACCESS.BOX, ADDKEY.BOX, GETKEY.BOX, and DELKEY.BOX modules contain all the data management routines that your program will need, and can be called from many different places in your program.

INPUT.INC

Similarly, you should have only one statement in your entire program that receives input from the user. This *read* statement should read a character variable from the keyboard:

```
Read(KBD, ch);                                              { ch : char }
```

For a good example of a string input routine, refer to procedure *InputStr* in the BTREE.PAS sample program on your distribution disk.

The same routine should be used to input both integer and real numbers. First, call your integer or real number input procedure and pass it two numeric parameters: the first is the integer or real number to be read, the second is the maximum number of digits (including minus signs and decimal point). This routine will then call the string input procedure. Next, use the Turbo Pascal *Val* procedure to convert the string to a number. Finally, test to see if the input is valid and proceed accordingly:

```
procedure InputStr(var s : MaxString; MaxLen : integer);
  { reads up to MaxLen characters into s }
    .
    .
    .
procedure Reject(Spaces : integer);
  { beeps and backspaces over invalid input }
    .
    .
    .
procedure StripLeadingSpaces(var s : MaxString);
  { deletes blanks until first non-blank character }
    .
    .
    .

procedure InputInteger(var ReadMe : integer;
                           MaxLen : integer);
var
  TempString : MaxString;
  Valid,TempLength : integer;
begin
  repeat
    InputStr(TempString, MaxLen);
    TempLength:=Length(TempString);
    Val(TempString, ReadMe, Valid);
    StripLeadingSpaces(TempString);
    if Valid <> 0 then
      Reject(TempLength));
    until Valid = 0;
  end;                                                  { InputInteger }
```

A similar procedure can be used to input real numbers. You can customize your string input routine to "know" when numbers are being entered and ignore non-numeric characters or decimal points on integer reads. Do this by passing a set of characters as a parameter that specifies characters that are legal to enter:

```
Integers:  ['0' .. '9', '-']
Reals:     ['0' .. '9', '-', '.']
All others: [' ' .. '~'] (non-numeric entry)
```

ERROR.INC

Every program should have a set of error handling procedures. The standard Turbo procedures *Exit* (version 3.0 and later) and *Halt* are powerful tools to use in your error routines. If a fatal error occurs in your program, you should pass an error message to an abort routine that displays the message and then exits the program:

```
procedure Abort(Message : MaxString);
begin
  GoToXY(1, 24);
  Writeln;
  Writeln(Message, '. Program aborting.');
  Halt;
end;                                              { Abort }
```

You might need a more sophisticated routine that can optionally close data or index files under certain circumstances. Error handling for a good database system is one of the most important features and requires careful planning.

Note: If you are using Turbo Pascal 3.0, you can write your own routine to handle I/O errors. See the *Turbo Pascal Reference Manual* and/or the READ.ME file on the Turbo Pascal distribution disk.

FILES.INC

This module contains routines that open and close the system. To open ACCESS data files, call the *OpenFile* or *MakeFile* procedures. When specifying the size of the record in this procedure call, be sure to use the *SizeOf* function:

```
OpenFile(DataFile, 'CUST.DTA', SizeOf(CustRec));
if OK then ...                     { always check OK after Turbo Access I/O operations }
```

If the size of the record in this statement is larger than *MaxDataRec* (or different from the record size of the data file), your program may be afflicted with a wide variety of seemingly inexplicable errors. If no error occurs and the file is saved, the data file will probably be corrupted. Therefore, you should inspect the constant declarations and the *MakeFile* and *OpenFile* statements to verify that the numbers correspond.

MAINT.INC, REPORTS.INC, MENU.INC

These modules are examples of routines common to many database programs and constitute "the real work" of the system. In this case, MAINT.INC contains all the routines to enter and edit data, REPORTS.INC has all the routines to print data on the printer, and MENU.INC controls the menu procedure that calls the other routines.

Designing Screen Output

Designing readable screen output is a very important part of your program development and deserves special mention here. From the "welcome" screen to the "good-bye" message, you should plan exactly what the user will see while your program is running.

Some of the most important considerations from the user's point of view are:

- Your screens must be uncluttered, logically organized and easy to read.

- The cursor should always be easy to locate, and its position should show the user exactly what type of input is required.

- Special areas of the screen should be set aside for helpful hints and error messages.
- Different screen displays should share the same style and conventions (boxes, wording, colors and highlighting).
- One special keystroke—for example, ESC—should abort the current process and return the user to the main menu.
- Online help should be available whenever possible.

Important considerations from a programmer's perspective are:

- You should be able to quickly write a routine that displays data on the screen by modifying an existing "template" routine.
- Colors, highlighting and screen coordinates for all special areas (help areas, error messages, menu entry fields) should all be declared as an array of records in the typed constant section of your program:

```
type
PositionRec = record
     x, y : byte;                                    { screen coordinates }
     HighLighting : boolean;                         { or specify colors  }
     end;                                            { PositionRec        }


     Positions = (CommandPos, HelpPos, ErrorPos);
     PositionArray =
          array[CommandPos..ErrorPos] of PositionRec;

const
PositionChart : PositionArray =
          ((x: 60;  y: 23;                           { CommandPos }
          Highlighting : True),
          (x:  1;  y: 24;                            { HelpPos    }
          Highlighting : False),
          (x:  1;  y:  1;                            { ErrorPos   }
          Highlighting : True ));
```

This type of program structure makes it easy to modify all screen displays in midstream. In addition, this code is very readable and can be easily modified for another system. It is best to place it in the declaration module or in a separate module of output routines.

- Designate a set of characters as special abort keys and declare them as a typed constant in your program:

```
const
    AbortSet : set of char = [^[, ^C];                           { ESC, Ctrl-C }
```

- Scan the keyboard during time-consuming operations (printouts, long computations, etc.) and look for these characters. When typed on the keyboard, one of these characters should abort the program, while another should simply return control to the main menu routine.

- If there is a lot of help text to be displayed, you might consider storing the text in a disk file. You can pass the help procedure a parameter that specifies what part of the file should be displayed at a given time.

By taking the time to design and implement a well-structured database program, you will ultimately save time in the debugging and modification stages of program development. In addition, this type of system can be easily changed to function as a "front end" for a completely different database manager. Consider these suggestions and refer to them when you are designing your program.

Appendix B
B+TREE STRUCTURE

This appendix provides an overview of the B+tree structure used by Turbo Access. Since Turbo Access handles the creation and maintenance of B+trees automatically, it isn't necessary for you to understand (or even read) the material in this appendix. However, if you are an experienced programmer, a deeper understanding of B+trees will enable you to fine-tune the Turbo Access system for your application programs. The information in this appendix can also help you set values for the constants used by Turbo Access (see Chapter 3).

A general discussion of tree structures is presented, followed by a discussion of B+trees in particular and how they are used by the Turbo Access system. Concepts such as roots, nodes, pages, leaves, items, and keys are also explained.

Trees: The Quickest Route is Not Always a Straight Line

Suppose you have a database consisting of customer names, telephone numbers, addresses, and billing status. When you ask your computer to find the telephone number of a customer, unless it is equipped with Turbo Access or something similar, it will search sequentially through each record one at a time. If that customer's telephone number happens to be at the bottom of the database file, it will take a good deal of time to find it.

Trees provide a way to search through lengthy data files quickly without looking at every record in the file. A tree is simply a way to organize data. Each piece of data can be represented by a *node* in the tree. There are three types of nodes: a *root node, internal nodes,* and *leaf nodes.* In a *binary tree,* each node can have zero, one, or two *children.* A *child* node is a node pointed to by a *parent* node, which is either a root node or an internal nodeF. A leaf node is a node that has no children. Thus, a tree is made up of nodes and pointers that connect the nodes (see Figure B-1).

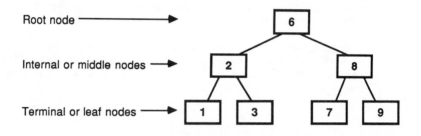

Figure B-1. A Binary Tree

To find a particular piece of data in the tree, the tree is searched one node at a time starting at the root node. At each node, there are four possibilities:

- The current node contains the data being sought.
- The data being sought is less than the current node, in which case the left child is the next node to be searched.
- The data being sought is greater than the current node, in which case the right child will be searched next.
- The current node does not contain the sought data and the node is a leaf; this means that the sought data is not in the binary tree.

Thus, when searching a binary tree, a decision is made at each node to discard or retain it, thereby eliminating half of the nodes under consideration. This makes tree searching efficient.

B + tree Fundamentals

Binary trees are efficient data structures for many purposes, but there are other, more efficient, data structures to handle large amounts of data. The Turbo Access system uses one such data structure called the *B+ tree*. (The *B* stands for R. Bayer, the inventor.)

The main difference between a B+ tree and a binary tree is that more than two children are allowed at each level.

A B+ tree's *pages* are analogous to a binary tree's nodes: There is a *root page*, *internal pages*, and *leaf pages*. Each page can contain several *items*. Each item holds an abbreviation of the data record. There are typically 16 items on a page.

Each root page and each internal page has one child page for each item on the page, plus one extra child page. Leaf pages have no children.

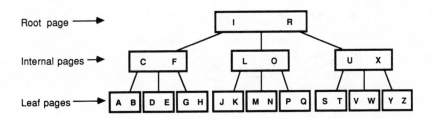

Figure B-2. A B+ tree

A sample B+tree is shown in Figure B-2. The items in the B+ tree are represented by letters and arranged alphabetically. There are two items on each page, and each page has three children. The items on each page are in alphabetical order (for example, R comes after I in the root page). The children are also ordered in that for each page, its first item is after every item on its first child page, and its second item is after every item on its second child page but before every item on the third child page. (For example, C is after A and B, and F is after D and E but before G and H.)

Searching a tree ordered in this manner can be very efficient. Similar to a binary tree, you start at the root, proceeding down the tree by making comparisons against the items within each page.

B+ trees are used to manage disk-stored databases too large to put in RAM. With Turbo Access, the data file is just one big array of records. Typically, there might be 5,000 records, with each record being 300 bytes. A separate file called an *index file* is used to organize the data into a B+ tree structure.

Manipulating entire data items is somewhat cumbersome; thus, in the index file each data record is abbreviated into a *key* and a *data reference*. A key is usually a portion of a data record that is sufficient to determine the ordering of the data records. A data reference is a pointer that indicates where the complete data record is stored. (These concepts are explained more fully in later sections.)

Turbo Access provides procedures for accessing, inserting, and deleting data records. Because it uses B+ trees, each operation involves a very small number of disk accesses and is very efficient.

Elements of a B+ tree

Trees are most efficient if the items are distributed fairly evenly throughout the tree; therefore, B+ trees are defined to ensure balance. Turbo Access routines automatically maintain these properties of B+ trees.

A B+ tree of *order n* is a tree that satisfies the following constraints:

- Excluding the root, all pages have at least *n* items.
- Each page has, at most, 2*n* items.
- A page is either a leaf with no active page references, or it has one page reference for each item plus one extra page reference.
- All leaf pages must be on the same *level*.
- Items on a page do not contain any data; they contain only keys and references to other pages and data records.

These constraints provide several advantages. First, they ensure that all parts of the B+ tree have a minimum information density; that is, at least 50 percent of the B+ tree consists of items. Secondly, most of the items have the same search-path length, which is the number of levels in the tree that a search would have to go through if it started at the root. The remainder of items have shorter paths.

Adding items to or deleting items from a B+ tree may cause the tree to become temporarily *unbalanced*. However, Turbo Access uses balancing algorithms to ensure that the previously described constraints are always satisfied.

With a B+ tree, a very large number of items can be put in a tree with a very small number of levels. For example, the maximum number of keys in the Turbo Access system is 65,535, or approximately 2 * *Max-Int*. If the B+ tree has order 16, then it will have, at most, four levels. Without the constraints on the B+ tree structure, the search path length would depend upon the history of key insertion and could become unacceptably large.

Keys

Each *item* of the B+tree holds a *key*. A *key* is a user-defined character string of 255 characters or less that is used to store and retrieve a record in a data file. A key can be formed from any word or code that is relevant to the data record the key is associated with. In most cases, a key is chosen from one or more of the *fields* in the data record. For example, to form a key for a customer database, the customer's first and last name could be concatenated to form a key of, say, length 25:

Fields	Data record #1	Data record #2
First name	'Jon'	'George'
Last name	'Jones'	'Washington'
Company	'Acme Supply'	'U.S. Government'
Etc.	...	...

```
         1         2
12345678901234567890012345
```

Key #1	'Jones Jon '
Key #2	'Washington George '

A string uses an ordering system that makes use of the relational operators ">", "=" and "<". (For a discussion of this ordering system, refer to the *Turbo Pascal Reference Manual: String Type.*) Since each key has a relative rank (according to its length and ASCII value) in the tree, the order of a given set of keys is fixed. In the previous example, two key strings might be identical and thus have the same rank. The Turbo Access system determines the rank of identical keys in one of two ways, depending on how the index file is created.

If the index file is created with a status of no duplicate keys allowed, then the system will warn the user program when an attempt is being made to add a duplicate key. The user program can then take appropriate action.

If the index file is created with a status of duplicate keys allowed, then adding two identical keys will cause the entries to be ordered by physical record number (which is *always* unique). In this case, if an attempt is made to delete a key, the system checks both the key itself and the record number associated with it to ensure that the correct key is deleted.

Both the RAM space required by B + tree procedures and the disk space used by index files grow with increasing key lengths. The key must be long enough to allow for a sufficient number of key variations to separate all entries in the index file. In many cases, abbreviating the original key information will serve the purpose.

For example:

Henry Smith, Plumber could be 'PlumSmitH'

Items

The fundamental unit of a B + tree is a record data type called an *item*. An item represents the connection between a key string and a physical data record (see Figure B-3), and is made up of a key string, a data reference, and a page reference.

The *key string* is used by Turbo Access to search the B + tree, the *data reference* points to the location in the data file where the data record associated with the key is found, and the *page reference* forms the link in the B + tree by pointing to a *page* where all keys are greater than the current item's key string.

The key string and the data reference are generated by the user program (that is, the key string from record fields and the data reference returned by the *AddRec* routine). The page reference is generated internally by the *AddKey* procedure.

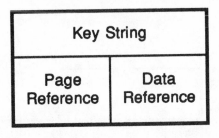

Key String	
Page Reference	**Data Reference**

Figure B-3. An Item

Pages

A unit or record of an index file is called a *page*. A page is a record containing three structures: an *array* of items, an *extra page reference*, and a *count* (see Figure B-4). In the Turbo Access system, the array has room for a fixed number of the items described in the previous section. This number is called the *page size*, and is exactly twice the order of the B + tree. It may be any even number between 4 and 254.

The number of items actually in a page can be anything between *page size*/2 and *page size* items. Since this number varies, each page must keep track of how many items it holds using the *count* field, which contains the number of items currently on the page. The count field always points to the last valid item in the array.

Since there is one page reference for each item, and the number of page references is one more than the number of items, there must be an *extra page reference*. The extra page reference is used to find keys with values that are less than any key on the current page.

For example, if a page contains items with keys X, Y, and Z, then the page reference associated with X points to a page with keys greater than X but less than Y. Likewise, the page reference associated with Y points to a page with keys greater than Y but less than Z, and the page reference associated with Z points to a page with keys greater than Z. The extra page reference points to a page with keys less than X.

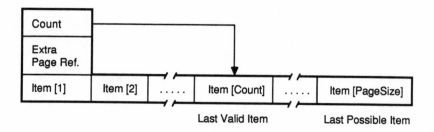

Last Valid Item   Last Possible Item

Figure B-4. Structure of a Page in an Index File

There are three distinct types of pages: the *root* page, the *internal* pages and the *leaf* pages.

The first page of the B+tree is called the *root page*, and may contain as little as one item. All other pages of the B+tree must be at least half full. This means that there are, at most, *page size* items and, at least, *page size*/2 items on all pages except the root page.

The *internal* pages always have between (*page size* + 1) and (*page size*/2 + 1) pointers to other pages. This keeps the B+tree balanced.

The *leaf* pages are at the bottom of the tree, and contain no active page references (that is, they do not have pointers to other pages).

How Pages are Organized into B+Trees

B+trees are constructed of pages. As shown in Figure B-5, each item holds a possible page reference for each key. In a B+tree, the page to which the page reference points contains additional items with keys. All of these keys are larger than the key associated with the page reference.

A search for a given key in a B+ tree follows a path that starts at the root page and jumps to a child page by following a page reference if the key is not on the page. The page references on each page are ordered so that the appropriate child page can be found by comparing the given key to the other keys on the page.

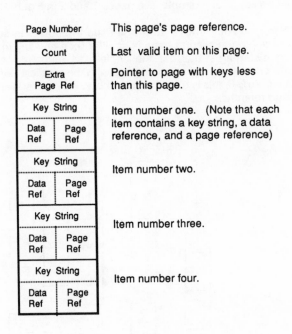

Figure B-5. The Page Structure

All paths in a B+tree start at the root page, and a jump can be made to a page with either larger or smaller keys. Keys are ordered in a B+tree so that each page in the tree can be reached by one—and only one—path. The number of jumps in a path is called the *level* of the page, with the root page being level one; the leaf pages have a level equal to the height of the B+tree.

For example, if an item contains the key *M*, (see root page in Figure B-6), that item's page reference will point to a page where all the items contain keys greater than *M* (for instance, *R* and *V*). Thus, consecutive jumps from a page item to that item's page reference follow a path of increasing keys. The path stops at the leaf page where there are no active page references. These jump decisions are always made by the Turbo Access system.

If a jump is made from an item's page reference, the search key must be larger than that item's key but smaller than the next item's key. After the jump is made, the search key could be smaller than all the keys on the new page. In this situation, the extra page reference is used. It points to another page where all the keys are smaller than that page's keys (for example, see pages 1 and 2 in Figure B-6).

Thus, you could move from one page to another in such a way that any key in the second page is smaller than any key in the first page. When starting at the root, the single path made from only extra page references will end at the leaf page with the smallest key in the B+ tree. In Figure B-6, this is page 1, since it contains the key A and has no extra page reference.

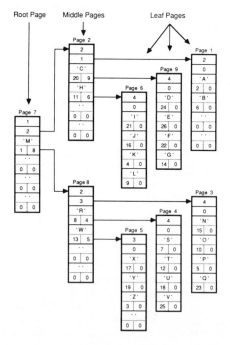

Figure B-6. Diagram of a B + tree of Order 2

Finding the Data Reference

Turbo Access locates a data record by using a specified key. The page with the data reference is found by following a path starting at the root page. If all keys on the page are larger than the key being sought, the next page to be investigated is referenced by the extra page reference. If this is not the case, the reference to the next page is found in the item with the largest key that is less than the key being sought. The search continues until the key is found, or until a leaf page is reached with no result.

The root page could be searched for a key with an ordinary search routine, however, Turbo Access uses a binary search. If the item is found, the associated data record can be read into memory with one disk access. If the key is not found on the root, the search continues on the page pointed to by the item's key closest to (but less than) the search key.

For example, if the root page contains the key entry M (see Figure B-6) and the search key is N, the page search will fail after the first comparison because the count variable will terminate the search. At this point, the search will continue on the page referenced by key M (see page 8 in Figure B-6). Since this page contains all keys greater than the search key, the next page to search is referenced by the extra page reference (see page 3 in Figure B-6). Searching this page yields the desired key; thus, the entire B+tree search is successful. The data record pointed to by the data reference in the item with key N (data record #13 in Figure B-7) can then be read into memory.

#1	Information for key 'M'
#2	Information for key 'A'
#3	Information for key 'Z'
#4	Information for key 'K'
#5	Information for key 'P'
#6	Information for key 'B'
#7	Information for key 'S'
#8	Information for key 'R'
#9	Information for key 'L'
#10	Information for key 'O'
#11	Information for key 'H'
#12	Information for key 'T'
#13	Information for key 'W'
#14	Information for key 'G'
#15	Information for key 'N'
#16	Information for key 'J'
#17	Information for key 'X'
#18	Information for key 'U'
#19	Information for key 'Y'
#20	Information for key 'C'
#21	Information for key 'I'
#22	Information for key 'F'
#23	Information for key 'Q'
#24	Information for key 'D'
#25	Information for key 'V'
#26	Information for key 'E'

Figure B-7. Data File Showing Order of Insertion

B + tree Administration

When data records are inserted or deleted from the data file, the corresponding keys must be inserted or deleted from the index file and the page items must be rearranged by the Turbo Access system. The following are examples of how Turbo Access inserts and deletes keys.

Inserting Keys

When a key is presented to the B+tree for insertion, the tree is checked to determine whether or not the key is already present. If the key is new or if duplicate keys are allowed, the search stops at a leaf page. If the leaf page is not full, the key is inserted into the page so that the page remains sorted. If the leaf page is full (that is, it already contains $2n$ items), a new page is added.

This process of adding new pages is called *page splitting*. The $2n+1$ keys are redistributed. The n largest items are moved to the new page, the n smallest items stay on the old page, and the middle item $(n+1)$ is moved to an *ancestral* page where it is associated with a reference to the new page. This scheme preserves the order of items in the B+ tree.

If the ancestral page is full, it must be split to accept the item moved from the leaf level. In this way, page splitting propagates recursively from the leaves all the way to the root. If the root page is split, a new root is created and the B+tree grows in height by one. Splitting the root page is the only way a B+ tree can grow in height.

Figure B-8 shows an example of how a B+ tree grows by repeated insertions. The B+ tree has order one in this case. Note that the properties of B+ trees and the ordering of items with the tree are maintained after each insertion. (The order of a Turbo Access B+tree is always at least two; this example is for illustrative purposes only.)

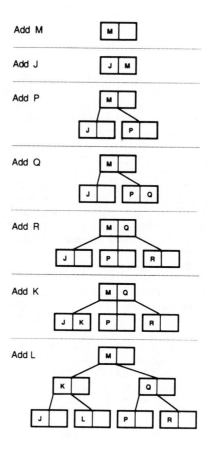

Figure B-8. How a B+tree Grows

Deleting Keys

When a key is to be deleted, Turbo Access finds its location in the tree. If the key is on a leaf page, it is simply removed. If the key is situated elsewhere in the tree, the process of deletion becomes more complicated. In this case it is necessary to replace the key with another key at the leaf level in the tree, while keeping the page reference associated with the deleted key.

Fortunately, it is always possible to find a suitable key that will not destroy the key order. The smallest key that is larger than the one to be deleted is always on a leaf page. Likewise, the largest key that is smaller than the one to be deleted is also always on a leaf page. One of these can be used to replace the deleted key without affecting key order.

It is possible that removing a key from a leaf page will leave the page with too few items (that is, less than n where n is the order of the B+ tree). In this case, Turbo Access uses a rebalancing method to redistribute the items. In simpler cases, an item is simply borrowed from an adjacent page. In more complicated cases, a process called *page merging* (analogous to page splitting) is used to merge pages. In an extreme case, page merging can propagate all the way to the root, reducing the number of levels in the B+ tree by one.

For more information on tree structures, refer to the following sources:

- Chaturvedi, Atindra. "Tree Structures," Parts 1, 2. *PC Tech Journal*, (Feb. and Mar. 1985).
- Horowitz, E., et al. *Fundamentals of Data Structure*. Pitman (1976).
- Knuth, Donald E. *The Art of Computer Programming*, Addison Wesley. Vol. 3 (1976).
- Wirth, Niklaus. *Algorithms + Data Structures = Programs*. Prentice Hall (1976).

Notes:

Appendix C
ASCII TABLE

DEC	HEX	CHAR	DEC	HEX	CHAR	DEC	HEX	CHAR	DEC	HEX	CHAR
0	00	^@NUL	32	20	SPC	64	40	@	96	60	'
1	01	^A SOH	33	21	!	65	41	A	97	61	a
2	02	^B STX	34	22	"	66	42	B	98	62	b
3	03	^C ETX	35	23	#	67	43	C	99	63	c
4	04	^D EOT	36	24	$	68	44	D	100	64	d
5	05	^E ENQ	37	25	%	69	45	E	101	65	e
6	06	^F ACK	38	26	&	70	46	F	102	66	f
7	07	^G BEL	39	27	'	71	47	G	103	67	g
8	08	^H BS	40	28	(	72	48	H	104	68	h
9	09	^I HT	41	29	)	73	49	I	105	69	i
10	0A	^J LF	42	2A	*	74	4A	J	106	6A	j
11	0B	^K VT	43	2B	+	75	4B	K	107	6B	k
12	0C	^L FF	44	2C	,	76	4C	L	108	6C	l
13	0D	^M CR	45	2D	-	77	4D	M	109	6D	m
14	0E	^N SO	46	2E	.	78	4E	N	110	6E	n
15	0F	^O SI	47	2F	/	79	4F	O	111	6F	o
16	10	^P DLE	48	30	0	80	50	P	112	70	p
17	11	^Q DC1	49	31	1	81	51	Q	113	71	q
18	12	^R DC2	50	32	2	82	52	R	114	72	r
19	13	^S DC3	51	33	3	83	53	S	115	73	s
20	14	^T DC4	52	34	4	84	54	T	116	74	t
21	15	^U NAK	53	35	5	85	55	U	117	75	u
22	16	^V SYN	54	36	6	86	56	V	118	76	v
23	17	^W ETB	55	37	7	87	57	W	119	77	w
24	18	^X CAN	56	38	8	88	58	X	120	78	x
25	19	^Y EM	57	39	9	89	59	Y	121	79	y
26	1A	^Z SUB	58	3A	:	90	5A	Z	122	7A	z
27	1B	^[ESC	59	3B	;	91	5B	[	123	7B	{
28	1C	^/ FS	60	3C	<	92	5C	\	124	7C	I
29	1D	^] GS	61	3D	=	93	5D	]	125	7D	}
30	1E	^^ RS	62	3E	<	94	5E	^	126	7E	~
31	1F	^_US	63	3F	?	95	5F	_	127	7F	DEL

Notes:

SUBJECT INDEX

A

ACCESS.BOX, 12, 13, 83, 85, 125
AddKey procedure, 17, 20, 32, 33, 35, 83, 94
  and duplicate keys, 94
ADDKEY.BOX, 13, 83, 125
AddRec procedure, 20, 29, 30, 95
ASCII table, 147
Assign procedure, 65

B

B+tree, 131ff
BTREE.PAS, 41ff

C

ClearKey procedure, 97
CloseFile procedure, 28, 98
CloseIndex procedure, 28, 99
Constants, 13, 85ff, 124
CUST.DAT, 42
CUST.IXC, 42
CUST.IXN, 42
CUSTOMER.DTA, 61ff, 84

D

Data file
  closing, 28, 98
  creating, 28, 108
  defined, 7
  large, 23
  length, 103
  opening, 28, 112
  record, see *record*
  routines, 95, 98, 102, 103, 106, 108, 112, 117, 120
  splitting, 23
DataFile type, 29, 85
Data item size, 60
Data reference
  defined, 16
  search, 137
Deleted data records, 40
  reuse, 21
DeleteKey procedure, 21, 39, 83, 100
DeleteRec procedure, 20, 24, 102
DELKEY.BOX, 13, 83, 125
Duplicate keys, 22
  and AddKey, 94
  and DeleteKey, 100
  and SearchKey, 118

E

Error handling, 18-19, 30, 65, 127
ERROR.INC, 127

F

FileLen function, 35, 36, 103
FILES.INC, 128
FindKey procedure, 20-21, 33-34, 37, 104

G

GETKEY.BOX, 13, 83, 125
GetMem procedure, 59-60
GetRec function, 20-21, 36, 38, 106
GINST
  general description, 2, 121ff
  routines, 85
GINST.COD, 85
GINST.COM, 85
GINST.DTA, 85
GINST.MSG, 85

I

Include statement, 12
Including modules in program, 83
Index file
  closing, 28, 99
  corrupted, 34

R

Record
  adding, 19, 29, 33, 94-95
  defined, 8
  defining, 25
  deleted, 21, 35
  deleting, 20, 39, 102
  size, 16
  size of, 29
  updating, 41
REPORTS.INC, 128
Reset procedure, 65
Root page, 133

S

SearchKey procedure, 20-21, 38,
  118, 147
  and duplicate keys, 118
SETCONST.PAS, 13, 124
SizeOf function, 15, 29, 33, 60, 127
SORT.BOX, 60ff, 85
SORT1.PAS, 60ff, 85
SORT2.PAS, 69ff, 85
Sorting, 58ff
  multiple keys, 75
STOCK.DTA, 69ff, 85
Str procedure, 22, 135-136
StrToInt function, 22

T

TalOcheck, 18, 85, 95
Terminal page
  see *Leaf page*
Terminating user program, 20
Turbo Access files
  ACCESS.BOX, 83
  ADDKEY.BOX, 83
  DELKEY.BOX, 83
  GETKEY.BOX, 83
Turbo Access programs,
  see *Program design*
Turbo Access, 5ff
  B+trees, 131ff
  constants, 85ff
  initialization, 18
  program structure, 17ff

Turbo Pascal 3.0, 12, 16
Turbo Sort, 2, 58ff
  memory management, 61
  memory requirements, 60
  routines, 84
TurboSort function, 84
Type
  DataFile, 29, 85
  IndexFile, 33, 85
  of keys, 135
Types, 85

U

Untyped parameter, 63, 66
UsedRecs function, 120
User program
  see *Program design*

V

Variable
  OK, 85
  system, 18
Virtual memory, 61

CATALOG OF BORLAND PRODUCTS

Available at better dealers nationwide. Call (800) 556-2283 for the dealer nearest you. To order by Credit Card call (800) 255-8008, CA (800) 742-1133

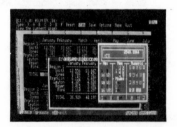

INCREASE YOUR PRODUCTIVITY
BY 50% OR YOUR MONEY BACK

SuperKey turns 1,000 keystrokes into 1!

Yes, SuperKey can *record* lengthy keystroke sequences and play them back at the touch of a single key. Instantly. Like Magic.

Say, for example, you want to add a column of figures in 1-2-3. Without SuperKey you'd have to type seven keystrokes just to get started. ["shift-@-s-u-m-shift-(")]. With SuperKey you can turn those 7 keystrokes into 1.

SuperKey keeps your 'confidential' files. . .CONFIDENTIAL!

Time after time you've experienced it: anyone can walk up to your PC, and read your confidential files (tax returns, business plans, customer lists, personal letters. . :).

With SuperKey you can encrypt any file, even while running another program. As long as you keep the password secret, only YOU can decode your file. SuperKey implements the U.S. government Data Encryption Standard (DES).

SuperKey helps protect your capital investment.

SuperKey, at your convenience, will make your screen go blank after a predetermined time of screen/keyboard inactivity. You've paid hard-earned money for your PC. SuperKey will protect your monitor's precious phosphor. . .and your investment.

SuperKey protects your work from intruders while you take a break.

Now you can lock your keyboard at any time. Prevent anyone from changing hours of work. Type in your secret password and everything comes back to life. . .just as you left it.

SUPERKEY is now available for an unbelievable $69.95 (not copy-protected).

Minimum System Configuration: SUPERKEY is compatible with your IBM PC, XT, AT, PCjr. and 100% compatible microcomputers. Your computer must have at least 128K RAM, one disk drive and PC-DOS 2.0 or greater.

REFLEX
THE ANALYST™

Reflex™ is the most amazing and easy to use database management system. And if you already use Lotus 1-2-3, dBASE or PFS File, you need Reflex—because it's a totally new way to look at your data. It shows you patterns and interrelationships you didn't know were there, because they were hidden in data and numbers. It's also the greatest report generator for 1-2-3.

REFLEX OPENS MULTIPLE WINDOWS WITH NEW VIEWS AND GRAPHIC INSIGHTS INTO YOUR DATA.

The FORM VIEW lets you build and view your database.

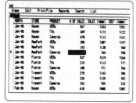

The LIST VIEW lets you put data in tabular List form just like a spreadsheet.

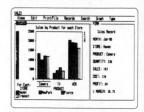

The GRAPH VIEW gives you instant interactive graphic representations.

The CROSSTAB VIEW gives you amazing "cross-referenced" pictures of the links and relationships hidden in your data.

The REPORT VIEW allows you import and export to and fro Reflex, 1-2-3, dBASE, PFS File a other applications and prints information in the formats you wa

So Reflex shows you. Instant answers. Instant pictures. Instant analysis. Instant understanding.

THE CRITICS' CHOICE:

"The next generation of software has officially arrived."
Peter Norton, PC WEEK

"Reflex is one of the most powerful database programs on the market. Its multiple views, interactive windows and graphics, great report writer, pull-down menus and cross tabulation make this one of the best programs we have seen in a long time . . .

The program is easy to use and not intimidating to the novice . . . Reflex not only handles the usual database functions such as sorting and searching, but also "what-if" and statistical analysis . . . it can create interactive graphics with the graphics module. The separate report module is one of the best we've ever seen."
Marc Stern, INFOWORL

Minimum System Requirements: Reflex runs on the IBM® PC, XT, AT and compatibles. 384K RAM minimum. IBM Color Graphics Adapter®, Hercules Monochrome Graphics Card™, or equivalent. PC-DOS 2.0 or greater. Hard disk and mouse optional. Lotus 1-2-3, dBASE, or PFS File optional.

BORLAND
INTERNATIONAL

Suggested Retail Price $99.95 (not copy-protected)

SIDEKICK ®

SideKick, the Macintosh Office Manager, brings information management, desktop organization and telecommunications to your Macintosh. Instantly, while running any other program.

A full-screen editor/mini-word processor lets you jot down notes and create or edit files. Your files can also be used by your favorite word processing program like MacWrite™ or MicroSoft® Word .

A complete telecommunication program sends or receives information from any on-line network or electronic bulletin board while using any of your favorite application programs. A modem is required to use this feature.

A full-featured financial and scientific calculator sends a paper-tape output to your screen or printer and comes complete with function keys for financial modeling purposes.

A print spooler prints *any* text file while you run other programs.

A versatile calendar lets you view your appointments for a day, a week or an entire month. You can easily print out your schedule for quick reference.

A convenient "Things-to-Do" file reminds you of important tasks.

A convenient alarm system alerts you to daily engagements.

A phone log keeps a complete record of all your telephone activities. It even computes the cost of every call. Area code hook-up provides instant access to the state, region and time zone for all area codes.

An expense account file records your business and travel expenses.

A credit card file keeps track of your credit card balances and credit limits.

A report generator prints-out your mailing list labels, phone directory and weekly calendar in convenient sizes.

A convenient analog clock with a sweeping second-hand can be displayed anywhere on your screen.

On-line help is available for all of the powerful SIDEKICK features.

Best of all, everything runs concurrently.

SIDEKICK, the software Macintosh owners have been waiting for.

SideKick, Macintosh's Office Manager is available now for $84.95 (not copy-protected).

Minimum System Configuration: SIDEKICK is available now for your Macintosh microcomputer in a format that is not copy-protected. Your computer must have at least 128K RAM and one disk drive. Two disk drives are recommended if you wish to use other application programs. A Hayes-compatible modem is required for the telecommunications function. To use SIDEKICK'S autodialing capability you need the Borland phone-link interface.

BORLAND
INTERNATIONAL

LEARN PASCAL FROM THE FOLKS WHO INVENTED TURBO PASCAL® AND TURBO DATABASE TOOLBOX®.

Borland International proudly introduces **Turbo Tutor**®. The perfect complement to your **Turbo Pascal** compiler. **Turbo Tutor** is *really* for everyone— even if you've never programmed before.

And if you're already proficient, **Turbo Tutor** can sharpen up the fine points. The 300 page manual and program disk divides your study of Pascal into three learning modules:

FOR THE NOVICE: Gives you a concise history of Pascal, tells you how to write a simple program, and defines the basic programming terms you need to know.

ADVANCED CONCEPTS: If you're an expert, you'll love the sections detailing subjects such as "how to use assembly language routines with your **Turbo Pascal** programs."

PROGRAMMER'S GUIDE: The heart of **Turbo Pascal.** This section covers the fine points of every aspect of **Turbo Pascal** programming: program structure, data types, control structures, procedures and functions, scalar types, arrays, strings, pointers, sets, files and records.

A MUST. You'll find the source code for all the examples in the book on the **accompanying disk** ready to compile.

Turbo Tutor may be the only reference on Pascal and programming you'll ever need!

TURBO TUTOR—A REAL EDUCATION FOR ONLY $34.95.
(not copy-protected)

*Minimum System Configuration: TURBO TUTOR is available today for your computer running TURBO PASCAL for PC-DOS, MS-DOS, CP/M-80, and CP/M-86. Your computer must have at least 128K RAM, one disk drive and PC-DOS 1.0 or greater, MS-DOS 1.0 or greater, CP/M-80 2.2 or greater, or CP/M-86 1.1 or greater.

TURBO *GRAPHIX* TOOLBOX™

HIGH RESOLUTION GRAPHICS AND GRAPHIC WINDOW MANAGEMENT
FOR THE IBM PC

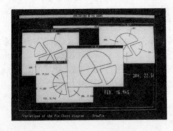

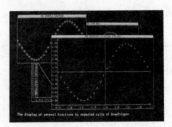

Dazzling graphics and painless windows.

The Turbo Graphix Toolbox™ will give even a beginning programmer the expert's edge. It's a complete library of Pascal procedures that include:

- Full graphics window management.

- Tools that allow you to draw and hatch pie charts, bar charts, circles, rectangles and a full range of geometric shapes.

- Procedures that save and restore graphic images to and from disk.

- Functions that allow you to precisely plot curves.

- Tools that allow you to create animation or solve those difficult curve fitting problems.

No sweat and no royalties.

You can incorporate part, or all of these tools in your programs, and yet, we won't charge you any royalties. Best of all, these functions and procedures come complete with source code on disk ready to compile!

John Markoff & Paul Freiberger, syndicated columnists:

"While most people only talk about low-cost personal computer software, Borland has been doing something about it. And Borland provides good technical support as part of the price."

Turbo Graphix Toolbox—only $54.95 (not copy protected).

Minimum System Configuration: Turbo Graphix Toolbox is available today for your computer running Turbo Pascal 2.0 or greater for PC-DOS, or truly compatible MS-DOS. Your computer must have at least 128K RAM, one disk drive and PC-DOS 2.0 or greater, and MS-DOS 2.0 or greater with IBM Graphics Adapter or Enhanced Graphics Adapter, IBM-compatible Graphics Adapter, or Hercules Graphics Card.

TURBO
EDITOR TOOLBOX

It's All You Need To Build Your Own Text Editor Or Word Processor.

Build your own lightning-fast editor and incorporate it into your Turbo Pascal programs. Turbo Editor Toolbox™ gives you easy-to-install modules. Now you can integrate a fast and powerful editor into your own programs. You get the source code, the manual and the know how.

Create your own word processor. We provide all the editing routines. You plug in the features you want. You could build a WordStar®-like editor with pull-down menus like Microsoft's® Word, and make it work as fast as WordPerfect™.

To demonstrate the tremendous power of Turbo Editor Toolbox, we give you the source code for two sample editors:

Simple Editor A complete editor ready to include in your programs. With windows, block commands, and memory-mapped screen routines.

MicroStar™ A full-blown text editor with a complete pull-down menu user interface, plus a lot more. Modify MicroStar's pull-down menu system and include it in your Turbo Pascal programs.

The Turbo Editor Toolbox gives you all the standard features you would expect to find in any word processor:

- Word wrap
- UNDO last change
- Auto indent
- Find and Find/Replace with options
- Set left and right margin
- Block mark, move and copy.
- Tab, insert and overstrike modes, centering, etc.

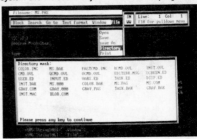

MicroStar's pull-down menus.

And Turbo Editor Toolbox has features that word processors selling for several hundred dollars can't begin to match. Just to name a few:

☑ **RAM-based editor.** You can edit very large files and yet editing is lightning fast.

☑ **Memory-mapped screen routines.** Instant paging, scrolling and text display.

☑ **Keyboard installation.** Change control keys from WordStar-like commands to any that you prefer.

☑ **Multiple windows.** See and edit up to eight documents—or up to eight parts of the same document—all at the same time.

☑ **Multi-Tasking.** Automatically save your text. Plug in a digital clock . . . an appointment alarm—see how it's done with MicroStar's "background" printing.

Best of all, **source code is included for everything in the Editor Toolbox.** Use any of the Turbo Editor Toolbox's features in your programs. And pay no royalties.

Minimum system configuration: The Turbo Editor Toolbox requires an IBM PC, XT, AT, 3270, PCjr or true compatible with a minimum 192K RAM, running PC-DOS (MS-DOS) 2.0 or greater. You must be using Turbo Pascal 3.0 for IBM and compatibles.

Suggested Retail Price $69.95
(not copy-protected)

BORLAND
INTERNATIONAL

HOW TO BUY BORLAND SOFTWARE